Elijah

MEN *of* CHARACTER

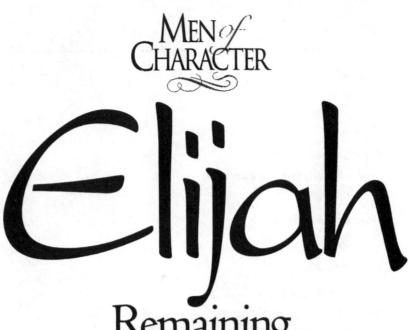

Elijah

Remaining Steadfast Through Uncertainty

GENE A. GETZ

Foreword by Paul Meier, M.D.

BROADMAN & HOLMAN PUBLISHERS

Nashville, Tennessee

Published by:
Broadman & Holman, Publishers
Nashville, Tennessee

Design: Steven Boyd

4261-66
0-8054-6166-3

Dewey Decimal Classification: 248.842
Subject Heading: Men \ Elijah \ Christian Life
Library of Congress Card Catalog Number: 94–40764

Unless otherwise noted, Scripture quotations are from the Holy Bible, New International Version, copyright © 1973, 1978, 1984 by International Bible Society. Passages marked NASB are from the New American Standard Bible, © the Lockman Foundation, 1960, 1962, 1963, 1968, 1971, 1972, 1973, 1975, 1977; used by permission.

Library of Congress Cataloging-in-Publication Data
Getz, Gene A.
   Elijah : remaining steadfast through uncertainty / Gene Getz.
   p. cm. — (Men of character)
   Rev. ed.
   Includes bibliographical references.
   ISBN 0-8054-6166-3
   1. Elijah. (Biblical figure) 2. Bible. O.T. Elijah—Criticism, interpretation, etc. I. Title. II. Series: Getz, Gene A. Men of character.
BS580.J7G47   1995
222'.2092—dc20
94–40764
CIP

2 3 4 5 99 98 97 96

*T*his book is dedicated to my good friends, Frank Minirth and Paul Meier, the two men who founded the Minirth-Meier New Life Clinics. Frank and Paul have been real encouragers to me personally and have assisted me often in helping people I minister to regain their physical, emotional, and spiritual health (Phil. 1:3).

Contents

Foreword

I've known Gene Getz personally for nearly twenty years, and I am very happy to consider him as a mentor, an inspiration, and a friend. In fact, my family and I attended the first Fellowship Bible Church that Gene started in the Dallas area— a ministry that has literally spread around the world. And when the original church launched a sister church, Richland Bible Fellowship, I became one of the founding elders.

However, I got to know Gene through his books several years before I moved to Dallas with my family. *Sharpening the Focus of the Church, Building Up One Another,* and *The Measure of a Man*—all books which have become classics—helped me to forge out my own philosophy of ministry and also impacted my approach to psychiatric counseling. The biblical principles Gene outlines are the very principles that make psychiatry a discipline that can bring healing to people's lives—particularly in terms of being a part of a functioning supportive fellowship. In fact, it was Gene that first introduced me to the small group ministry in the church (which we call minichurches)—an approach which has become an important part of my own life. Over the years, Gene has also become a real encouragement to me both by his courageous example in times of adversity and also by his warm words of personal encouragement.

This book on Elijah represents Gene's approach to the study and personal application of Scripture. He gets right down "inside of this man" and demonstrates that Elijah was indeed a mighty man of God, but also a "man just like us."

The chapters on Elijah's bout with depression and the principles God used to bring healing to his life will give you profound insights and encouragement. As a Christian psychiatrist, I could wish that all counselors understood these principles and used them in their practices as well as in their own lives.

I consider it a great privilege to recommend this book to every Christian man. And, if you're a woman, you'll enjoy it too! It will give you insights into men—how they think and how they function—to help you relate more effectively to all of us who make up the male species.

Paul Meier, M.D.
Cofounder,
Minirth-Meier New Life Clinics

A Man Just Like Us

*E*lijah is one of the men of the Bible who, once you meet him and get to know him, you'll never forget him. On the one hand, he did great exploits for God that are almost beyond our comprehension. His prayers of faith are unequaled. His boldness in proclaiming God's message reminds us of the apostle Paul! His determination to serve God and do His will makes Romans 12:1–2 come alive with meaning.

But Elijah was also a "man just like us" (James 5:17). He experienced intense fear and deep loneliness. At times, he doubted God's faithfulness. He allowed his anger to distort his thinking. He experienced such dark depression that he wanted to die!

In spite of his humanness, God used Elijah to demonstrate to all Israel that idolatry is a sinful practice that will bring divine judgment. No true "son of Abraham" will ever forget Elijah.

God honored Elijah by taking him to heaven without experiencing death and then allowing him to appear with Jesus Christ on the mount of transfiguration.

I'm eager to meet this man personally. Someday I will, but fortunately, I haven't had to wait until eternity to discover those qualities that made him truly a man of God. And neither do you.

Join me in this exciting study! No matter what your age, your vocation, your circumstances in life—whether married or single—you can learn lessons from Elijah that will transform the rest of your life! If you take this study seriously, you'll never be the same again! I guarantee it.

Chapter 1

Idolatry Comes in All Shapes and Sizes

Read 1 Samuel 8 and 1 Kings 16:29–17:1

When my wife, Elaine, and I were ministering in Hong Kong, we often saw people bow down to idols. Since only a small percentage of the population even claims to be Christian, the majority of these people are still involved in pagan worship. Their temples and shrines are filled with hundreds of images. Many people have household gods placed outside the entrance to their homes or inside on "god shelves." They believe these idols will bring them peace, protection, and prosperity.

Witch Doctors in Guatemala

I'll never forget our visit to several church structures while ministering in Guatemala. Though we had often heard how people in various parts of the world mix Christianity with pagan religions, we were shocked to see witch doctors performing idolatrous incantations in the main sanctuary of one of these churches.

Earlier, Elaine and I had visited a cave on a mountainside just outside that particular town. The inside walls of the cave were black from the smoke of burnt offerings. The floor was strewn with the remains of animals—chicken feathers, bones, etc. Christian crosses were crudely sketched on the soot-covered walls. This place was well-known in the community as a "witch doctor's cave"—a place where these men engaged in ceremonial rites, praying to evil spirits, and, at the same time, "worshiping" the cross of Christ.

It was startling enough to see Christianity and paganism practiced as a unified religion in a cave on a mountainside, but when we saw it practiced inside a "Christian" church building, it was even more shocking. Seeing this firsthand also helped us to understand more clearly how the children of Israel blended their old idolatrous habits with the worship of the one true God. This is called syncretism, and it is still prevalent in many parts of the world.

A Man Who Suddenly Appeared

God commissioned the prophet Elijah to confront idolatry in Israel. Without background or fanfare, he suddenly appears on the pages of the Old Testament. He's simply identified as "Elijah the Tishbite, from Tishbe in Gilead" (1 Kings 17:1).

We know nothing about Elijah's parents and his early years, and we can only speculate regarding his prophetic activity prior to this moment in his life. We can't even pinpoint the place where he was born. Archaeologists have never been able to identify with certainty the location of Tishbe, Elijah's hometown.

In some respects, this is rather startling since Elijah is very prominent in the New Testament. In fact, it was Elijah—along with Moses—who "appeared in glorious splendor, talking with Jesus" on the mount of transfiguration (Luke 9:31; Matt. 17:3). This is one of the most important events in biblical history. God the Father spoke directly and specifically to Peter, James, and John about His Son Jesus Christ. Embodied in this miraculous revelation is the essence of Christianity—the incarnation (God becoming a man), the death, burial, and resurrection of Christ, and His ascension back to the Father after having completed His work on earth.

"Greatness by Association"

Since Moses is identified as the greatest Old Testament prophet who ever lived (see Exod. 34:10), being selected to stand alongside him on the mount of transfiguration demonstrates Elijah's prominence in biblical history. We've all heard the phrase "guilt by association." "In this event, it was definitely *"greatness* by association."

There are many similarities between Elijah and his forefather, Moses. Both had unusual communication with God. Both were uniquely used by God to demonstrate His mighty power with signs and wonders and miracles. Both played a strategic role in Israel's spiritual direction. In fact, C. F. Keil states: "No other prophet, either before or after, strove and worked in the idolatrous kingdom for the honor of the Lord of Sabbath with anything like the same mighty power of God as the mighty prophet Elijah."[1]

But There Is a Striking Difference!

We're given a lot of information about Moses and his early years and his preparation to be involved in Israel's destiny. By contrast, we have virtually no knowledge about Elijah until he suddenly marched into Ahab's court and said, "As the LORD, the God of Israel, lives, whom I serve, there will be neither dew nor rain in the next few years except at my word" (1 Kings 17:1).

What an Awesome Mission!

It's impossible to comprehend the magnitude of Elijah's task unless we understand the events leading up to this confrontation.

Israel's Persistent Failures

God gave the nation Israel their first king because they wanted to be like other nations (see 1 Sam. 8:7). Though it displeased the Lord, He consented to give them their wish.

Saul served as their first king, followed by David and then David's son, Solomon. Even though this was not within God's perfect plan for Israel, He still extended His grace and promised His chosen people that if they obeyed Him, He would still bless them as a nation. If they did not, then He would curse them and scatter them to the ends of the earth (see Deut. 28:1–68).

As happened so frequently among many of Israel's leaders, a good beginning ended tragically. Solomon sinned against the Lord, particularly by marrying pagan women, which resulted in his worshiping their false gods. As God forewarned, judgment fell.

A Divided Kingdom

God dethroned Solomon, and the kingdom split. The northern tribes continued to be called "Israel" and the southern tribes (Judah and Benjamin) were ruled by Rehoboam. With very few exceptions, each northern and southern king followed in Solomon's footsteps. The children of Israel in both kingdoms continued to follow false gods and to commit horrible immorality.

Flagrant Idolatry

When Ahab, a "northern king," arrived on the scene, he "did more evil in the eyes of the LORD than any of those before him" (1 Kings 16:30). What a disgraceful way to be remembered in Israel's history!

Ahab married Jezebel, daughter of Ethbaal, who was king of the Sidonians. Her father was also a pagan priest and she followed in her father's footsteps. Jezebel's evil reputation was so notorious that Jesus Christ used her name many years later when He wrote a letter to the church in Thyatira: "You tolerate *that woman Jezebel,* who calls herself a prophetess. By her teaching she misleads my servants into sexual immorality and the eating of food sacrificed to idols" (Rev. 2:20).*

---

* Hereafter, italicized words in Scripture quotations indicate the author's emphases.

The "Sins of Jeroboam"

When Ahab became king, the Scriptures record that he "considered it *trivial* to commit the *sins of Jeroboam*" (1 Kings 16:31). To understand this unusual comparison—and the extent of Ahab's wickedness—let's look for a moment at Jeroboam's sins.

His Rise to Power

When Rehoboam succeeded his father, Solomon, as king, Jeroboam also emerged as a strong contender. Ironically, God had promised him ten tribes because of Solomon's sins. It happened. Ten tribes followed Jeroboam and the people of Judah and Benjamin followed Rehoboam.

Even though Jeroboam had proved himself to be a strong leader, even when he had served in Solomon's court (see 11:28), he was afraid that if the children of Israel continued to go to Jerusalem to worship, they eventually would "give their allegiance to . . . Rehoboam" (12:27). Consequently, he developed an evil plan to keep from losing power.

Golden Calves

To achieve his goal, Jeroboam changed the central place of worship. He set up two golden calves in Bethel and Dan and told the people that this change was for their convenience. "It is too much for you to go up to Jerusalem," he explained. "Here are your gods, O Israel, who brought you up out of Egypt" (v. 28). At this point, Jeroboam completely ignored the lesson that all Israel should have learned when Aaron had set up a golden calf at the base of Mount Sinai (see Exod. 32:31–35).

Jeroboam Led the Way

Jeroboam committed even more grievous sins. He "built shrines on high places and appointed priests from all sorts of people, even though they were not Levites"—a direct violation of God's commands (1 Kings 12:31). He not only instructed the children of Israel to worship these false gods, but he also modeled it with his own life. He "offered sacrifices on the altar. . . . sacrificing to the calves he had made" (v. 32).

Ahab's Greater Sin

Even though Jeroboam had committed an extremely destructive sin by establishing these new places of worship and setting up false gods, Ahab considered his actions as "trivial." Ahab's idolatry was worse. Though the "golden calves" Jeroboam erected were Egyptian symbols and "graven images" and an abomination to God, the people at least thought these idols would assist them in worshiping Jehovah. But Robert Jamieson reminds us that Ahab introduced Israel to the "heathen or Phoenician idols, Baal and Ashtaroth," and built "sanctuaries to them."[2] Though Jeroboam's idolatrous syncretism was abominable in the sight of God, Ahab's gods actually *replaced* Jehovah!

Elijah's Awesome Task!

It is against this historical backdrop that Elijah's awesome mission comes into clear focus. King Ahab had done "more to provoke the LORD, the God of Israel, to anger than did all the kings of Israel before him" (16:33). When Elijah marched into his presence to proclaim God's judgment, he faced a wicked and evil man who had led Israel further astray than any of his predecessors.

A Powerful "One-Liner"

Elijah's prophetic message was crisp, concise, and very clear! It's probably the most powerful "one line" message delivered by anyone in Israel's history. Elijah simply stated, *"There will be neither dew nor rain in the next few years except at my word"* (17:1c).

In actuality, we have no way of knowing if Elijah prefaced these words with any other remarks or if he dialogued with

Ahab following the pronouncement. Personally, I don't think he did. I believe he courageously walked into Ahab's presence, delivered this powerful message, and turned and walked out!

Neither are we told *how* Elijah delivered his message. Did he raise his voice? Did he shout? Did he point his finger? Did he deliver this prophetic message through tears? I believe he simply relayed his message in a straightforward, calm, somber voice. Whatever the "delivery system," Ahab definitely heard what Elijah said.

Was This a *Specific* Message from God?

In most instances in Scripture when prophets were about to speak directly for God, their message was introduced with the following statement: "The word of the LORD came to. . . ." Not so in this instance! Rather, the Scriptures simply state that Elijah had an audience with Ahab and made his pronouncement. We're not told that Elijah had received this message directly from God for this particular occasion. He only declared, "As the LORD, the God of Israel, lives, whom I serve, there will be neither dew nor rain in the next few years except at *my word*" (17:1).

God's Word to Moses

Why didn't the author of 1 Kings introduce this prophetic statement with the phrase "The word of the LORD came to Elijah. . . ."? Is it possible that Elijah had no specific word from God regarding what was about to happen? Admittedly, this is a speculative question. However, we can always engage in some "sanctified imagination" by reminding ourselves that God had already spoken to Israel regarding what would transpire if they committed this kind of idolatry. Look at what Moses said when he reviewed the Law before they entered the promised land:

> Be careful, or you will be enticed to turn away and worship other gods and bow down to them. Then the LORD's anger will burn against you, and he will *shut the heavens so that it will not rain* and the ground will yield no produce, and you

will soon perish from the good land the LORD is giving you. (Deut. 11:16–17; see also Lev. 26:19–20; Deut. 28:23–24)

Is This a Step of Faith Based on Prior Revelation?

We can now raise another question. Did Elijah pray and ask God to withhold rain from the earth based on God's earlier message to Moses? From what James wrote in the New Testament, this is a possibility. "Elijah was a man just like us. He prayed earnestly that it would not rain, and it did not rain on the land for three and a half years" (James 5:17).

If it's true that Elijah did not get a specific word from the Lord regarding the judgment that was about to come, it tells us a great deal about this man's faith in the living God. Elijah obviously knew what God had said years earlier to Moses— that *if Israel turned to false gods, He would indeed withhold rain from the earth.* It's possible that Elijah simply proceeded to confront Ahab based on what he already knew God said He would do under these circumstances.

What Motivated Elijah?

What would drive a man to speak as Elijah spoke—to do what Elijah did? After all, he "was a man just like us." He had the same emotions, experienced the same fears, and faced the same doubts as we all do. He certainly knew in his heart before he entered Ahab's court that he and his message would be rejected. Furthermore, he had to know this bold step would put his own life in jeopardy.

He Believed God

It's very apparent from Elijah's overall life story that he was motivated by his supernatural perspectives. He believed in a God who lived and who was true to His Word. He was definitely a man of faith. He had confidence in what God had already stated to Moses years before—that He would withhold rain from the earth and turn it "into dust and powder" if Israel followed false gods (Deut. 28:24).

God's chosen people were horribly guilty of the worst forms of idolatry. Elijah believed that God would honor prayer that is based on His revealed will! Before he ever entered Ahab's presence he had "prayed earnestly that it would not rain" and—as James recorded years later—"it did not rain on the land for three and a half years" (James 5:17). God certainly honored Elijah's faith!

He Served God

Elijah was also a dedicated man. He served the living God of Abraham, Isaac, and Jacob. Ahab couldn't miss this point, for Elijah had said, "As the LORD, the God of Israel, lives, *whom I serve*" (1 Kings 17:1b)! With this declaration Elijah was comparing the *living* God with Ahab's gods of wood and stone.

In essence this prophet was saying, "Ahab, you serve dead gods! I serve a God who is alive!" Unknown to Ahab, Elijah was also declaring, "God Himself will prove this point!" And as we'll see, this is exactly what happened!

When God Became Flesh

When Jesus Christ arrived on planet earth, the Greek and Roman cultures of the first century were permeated with idolatry. Many who became Christians were deeply involved in idol worship. Ironically, the Jews who lived at that time were relatively free from idolatry. Apparently, they had learned their lesson well from their history, whereas idolatry was the norm among the Gentiles.

"Man-Made Gods Are No Gods at All"

The apostle Paul "was greatly distressed" when he came to Athens and saw "that the city was *full of idols*" (Acts 17:16). It was there he proclaimed that the "Unknown God" they worshiped could be "known." He was not a god of wood and stone (see vv. 23–29).

Later, this great Apostle to the Gentiles created a serious riot in Ephesus because he taught "that *man-made gods* are no gods at all" (Acts 19:26). Those who molded these idols and sold them in the marketplace were livid with anger because Paul's teaching cut into their business. When many of these people became Christians, they stopped worshiping idols—and they stopped spending their money on these false gods.

Another example involves the Thessalonians. They, too, "turned to God from *idols to serve the living and true God*" (1 Thess. 1:9). Their lives were dramatically changed. Furthermore, they became a wonderful model to other believers throughout Macedonia and Achaia. Their *"faith in God* [had] become known everywhere" (v. 8).

Making the Transition

The gospel of Jesus Christ penetrated the idolatrous environment all over the first-century world. Many people turned to the God of Abraham, Isaac, and Jacob. However, sometimes this decision created some unusual problems. For example, the Corinthians had to be instructed as to what to do with meat that was sold in the marketplace that had already been offered to idols. Paul dealt with this problem very specifically in his first letter to the Corinthians believers (see 1 Cor. 8:1–13). Though the meat was all right by itself, Paul cautioned these believers to be sensitive to those Christians who were weak in their faith and who might fall back into idolatry by eating meat that had been offered to idols. "Be careful," he wrote, "that the exercise of your freedom does not become a stumbling block to the weak" (v. 9). As we move from the New Testament to the history of the church throughout the ages, it's apparent that idolatry has been a problem for thousands of years. But, wherever God's true message has gone, it has confronted this evil practice head-on. Bowing down to idols of wood and stone is definitely incompatible with serving the living and true God.

Two Thousand Years Later

For those of us who are Christians living in the western world, it's difficult to identify with idolatry as it was practiced in biblical cultures—as well as the way it is still practiced in some societies today. Most of us consider bowing down to idols made of wood and stone a primitive experience. Yet, as stated at the beginning of this chapter, great sections of the world's population still engage in this kind of flagrant idolatry.

Christianity and Idolatry

There is a reason why some branches of Christianity are more susceptible to syncretism—that is, blending pagan practices with Christian worship. For years, statuary and images have been a prominent part of certain branches of the Christian religion. Though many people who claim to be followers of Jesus Christ would vehemently deny bowing down to idols, it's a very natural thing for people who have worshiped pagan idols to adopt these "Christian" symbols and integrate them into their own religious system.

This is not a new problem for God's children. This is exactly what happened at Mount Sinai when Israel made a golden calf to represent God. They integrated their new faith into their old idolatrous practices. And this is what Jeroboam did, which Ahab considered trivial. However, it was not trivial to God.

This is why He thundered from Sinai and said:

> "You shall not make for yourself an idol in the form of anything in heaven above or on the earth beneath or in the waters below. You shall not bow down to them or worship them; for I, the LORD your God, am a jealous God, punishing the children for the sin of the fathers to the third and fourth generations of those who hate me." (Exod. 20:4–5)

"Is It Really True?"

Most American Christians would be shocked at what we saw in Guatemala. On one occasion, I was telling this story and related that I had not only seen witch doctors inside the church building offering pagan sacrifices to Christian statuary, but the local minister was outside in the local courtyard conducting mass. One person in the audience came up afterwards in a state of shock. He had great difficulty believing that I was actually stating facts. This, of course, I understand. It is shocking! But what I had shared was true—my wife and I saw it with our own eyes!

Unfortunately, this kind of syncretism is happening all over the world. People who profess to follow Christ often accept the teachings of Christianity as just another way to supplement their own pagan religious beliefs.

But what about those of us who would never practice the kind of idolatry I've just described? Is it possible that we, too, are just as guilty of a more subtle form of idol worship?

Humanistic Gods

Paul reminded us in his Roman letter that when man departs from God's will in worship, his first step is to exchange "the glory of the immortal God for images made to look like mortal man" (Rom. 1:23). Whenever and wherever this happens, Paul explained that we have "exchanged the truth of God for a lie, and worshiped and served *created things* rather than the Creator" (v. 25).

Elvis and Company

In our culture today, rather than worshiping *images* of people, we are more likely to worship *people*. Think for a moment about Elvis Presley. Though he died a number of years ago, there are people who still think he is alive. They've done incredible things to demonstrate their loyalty to a man who lived a self-destructive lifestyle. Years later, people of all ages are still "worshiping" his memory.

The same could be said of many other musicians, movie stars, athletes, and other prominent people. In America we tend to glorify these individuals.

Trash in the Media

In recent years, the more sordid the lifestyle, the more attention people get in the press, on radio, and on television.

TV shows reek with stories of the worst sorts of immorality. Radio talk show hosts shock people with discussions that not too many years ago would have been censored. X-rated movie stars parade their lifestyle before a watching world. Today these prominent personalities are becoming incredibly wealthy by writing books and producing videos that display their sexual exploits and deviant behavior.

Cult Leaders

On the religious side, we often worship cult leaders. Take the Moonies as a classic example, or those who committed mass suicide with Jim Jones. And what about the Branch Davidians?

These are extreme cases you say. I agree. But it is happening. And what about Bible-believing Christians who border on "pastor worship"? In the minds of some people, those who lead them can become more important than the God they represent. When this happens, we, too, are serving humanistic gods. And those of us in positions of authority are encouraging idolatry when we directly or indirectly allow this to happen.

Materialistic Gods

Jesus said, "No one can serve two masters. Either he will hate the one and love the other, or he will be devoted to the one and despise the other. You cannot serve both God and Money" (Matt. 6:24).

Millionaires on Strike

Our American society is a prime environment where people from all walks of life are serving materialistic gods. Greed is rampant. Even those who do not claim to be Bible-believing Christians recognize this blight in our society. How tragic when some of the highest-paid people in the world—namely, athletes—go out on strike because they want more money! Some of their complaints may be understandable—but frankly, I have a very difficult time accepting this behavior as legitimate. It appears to be a classic symptom of the cancerous-like disease that plagues our American culture. It's called "material-ism" but the Bible calls it idolatry.

Unfortunately, Christians also contract this disease. It's very contagious—and can even go unnoticed in our lives until it withers our souls and saps our spiritual strength.

Jesus offers the antidote to this disease: "But seek first His kingdom and His righteousness; and all these things shall be added to you" (Matt. 6:33, NASB).

A Challenge

Recently, when speaking on Jacob's life, I asked my own congregation about anything in their homes that might be a "household god." I used this illustration: Do you have any-thing in your home that is a luxury that keeps you from giving regularly and systematically to the Lord? For example, do you pay a monthly fee for cable television—and yet you don't have enough money to tithe? If that is indeed your situation, has that not become a household god? I personally believe it has. When this happens, we are guilty of idolatry.

Apply this illustration to all of the other luxuries in your home—including the car you drive. Have you obligated your-self to anything that you could do without that keeps you from giving your firstfruits to God? If you have, you're idol is materialism. Fortunately, you can do something about that. All you need do is make some choices. Thankfully, God will help you make the right choices.

Sensual Gods

Throughout history, idolatry and sexual immorality have always been closely aligned. Need we elaborate on what is happening in the American culture? More and more we are worshiping at the shrine of sex. We bow down to American sex symbols—both men and women—actually enjoying their fla-grant immorality. We are a nation preoccupied with sex. This, too, is idolatry.

Writing to the Ephesians, Paul said, "No immoral, impure or greedy person—*such a man is an idolater*—has any inheritance in the kingdom of Christ and of God" (Eph. 5:5).

Relational Gods

Ironically, at a time when marriages are breaking up, when parents are abandoning children, and children are dishonoring their parents, there are those who have made their family relationships and friendships more important than God. Jesus said, "Anyone who loves his father or mother more than me is not worthy of me; anyone who loves his son or daughter more than me is not worthy of me; and anyone who does not take his cross and follow me is not worthy of me" (Matt. 10:37–38).

Failure on the Home Front

Obviously, our children are very important. To fail in our family life is to fail miserably. In fact, it is one of the requirements for being a spiritual leader in the church. Paul stated that an elder or pastor "must be one who manages his own household well, keeping his children under control with all dignity (but if a man does not know how to manage his own household, how will he take care of the church of God?)" (1 Tim. 3:4–5, NASB).

The Peril of the Pendulum

Isn't it strange how easy it is to go from one extreme to another—in all areas of our lives. In some instances, we're experiencing an overreaction in family relationships. For years, many Christian parents neglected their children by being overly involved in spiritual activities. Their children rebelled and developed resentments toward God and the church. This, of course, is a tragedy. But, in some situations today, Christians have gone to the other extreme. They allow nothing—including God—to interfere with their relationships with family and friends. Both reactions, of course, are wrong!

It's possible to put both God and family and friends in proper perspective.

Becoming God's Man Today

Principles to Live By

To what extent are you guilty of syncretism in your Christian life? There are two ways to guard against idolatry in any form.

Principle 1. We must make right choices.

Joshua sets a beautiful example in making choices. Standing before the children of Israel, just before they were to settle in the promised land, he said:

> "Now fear the LORD and *serve him* with all faithfulness. Throw away the gods your forefathers worshiped beyond the River and in Egypt, and *serve the LORD.* But if *serving the LORD* seems undesirable to you, then *choose for yourselves this day* whom you will *serve,* whether the gods your forefathers *served* beyond the River, or the gods of the Amorites, in whose land you are living." (Josh. 24:14–15a)

Joshua culminated this powerful exhortation with a personal testimony—*"But as for me and my household,"* he said, *"we will serve the LORD"* (v. 15b).

We, too, must make this choice. And when we do, we must still be on guard against idolatry. We need to renew our commitment day by day to serve the living and true God. If we don't, we'll get subtly trapped in some form of idolatry.

Principle 2. We must look carefully at how we live our lives in the light of God's eternal Word.

After living a carnal life for years, Jacob had an encounter with God. The Lord told him to return to Bethel—the place where he had first met God when he was running away from his brother, Esau, after having deceived his father and stolen his brother's birthright (see Gen. 28:10–23).

Jacob had matured in his personal life and as a leader of his family. Following God's charge to return to Bethel, he issued an order to his whole household: "Put away the *foreign gods* which are among you, and purify yourselves and change your garments" (35:2, NASB).

Becoming a Man Who Makes Right Choices

Do you have any "foreign gods" you should get rid of? Is there anything in your life that is consistently more important than God and His will? Consider the following areas. Pray and ask the Holy Spirit to impress on your heart one area where you need to make a right choice. Then write a specific goal. For example, you may be putting the car you drive ahead of the God you claim to worship. You now realize your automobile has become your "god."

- Your own personal needs
- Your status and position
- Your material possessions
- Your recreational activities
- Television and movies
- Your job
- Your leisure time
- Your hobbies
- Other things:_____

Set a Goal

With God's help, I will begin immediately to carry out the following goal in my life:

_____

_____

_____

_____

Memorize the Following Scripture

But seek first his kingdom and his righteousness, and all these things will be given to you as well.

MATTHEW 6:33

Chapter 2

A Place to Hide

Read Daniel 3 and 6 and 1 Kings 17:4–6

God is—and always has been—in the business of protecting His servants from their enemies when they take a stand against idolatry. This happened again and again throughout biblical history.

The Fiery Furnace

Consider Daniel's three friends—Shadrach, Meshach, and Abednego. They defied an order issued by King Nebuchadnezzar to bow down to a towering idol, knowing that he had commanded that anyone who did "not fall down and worship" this massive, ninety-foot image would "immediately be thrown into a blazing furnace" (Dan. 3:6).

Nebuchadnezzar was furious! But since they had served him faithfully, he summoned the three men to appear before him to explain why they were defying his order. "Is it true, Shadrach, Meshach and Abednego," the king asked, "that you do not serve my gods or worship the image of gold I have set up?" (v. 14).

Uncertain of their future on this earth, but without wavering in their faith, these men acknowledged it was true but didn't defend their stand. "If we are thrown into the blazing furnace," they said, *"the God we serve* is able to save us from it, and he will rescue us from your hand, O king" (v. 17).

God chose to deliver these men against insurmountable odds. Demonstrating the fury that raged in his own soul, Nebuchadnezzar ordered that the furnace be heated seven times hotter than usual. In fact, it was so red with heat that the men who threw Shadrach, Meshach, and Abednego into the blazing inferno were overcome by the flames and lost their own lives.

Imagine the look on the king's face when he looked into the furnace and saw "four men walking around in the fire, unbound and unharmed." Stunned by what he saw, he shouted, "Look! . . . The fourth looks like a son of the gods" (v. 25).

Nebuchadnezzar probably saw an Old Testament appearance of Jesus Christ. Without knowing it, he was looking not at a son of the gods but at *the Son of God!* God miraculously protected these men who stood so firmly against idolatry.

The Familiar Lion's Den

Years later, the Lord once again demonstrated His faithfulness—this time to Daniel. Falling prey to a diabolical scheme designed to tap his huge ego, King Darius had issued a decree—for a certain period of time—that if anyone prayed to any god or man rather than to him, he would be thrown into a den of lions (see 6:7). Like his three friends, Daniel ignored the king's decree and continued his practice of getting down on his knees and praying three times a day to the living God.

Darius was overcome with grief because of what had happened. He admired and respected Daniel; however, he had issued an irreversible decree. What may be surprising, he actually believed—and admitted—that Daniel's God would protect him.

The Lord sent an angel (probably another Old Testament appearance of Jesus Christ) who "shut the mouths of the lions" (v. 22). Overwhelmed, Darius released Daniel unharmed and destroyed the men who had "set him up" to carry out this terrible deed.

Years Before

Long before Daniel and his three friends lived, Elijah had already proven God's faithfulness. Who knows? Perhaps it was Elijah's sterling example of faith that gave Daniel and his three friends courage to refuse to worship false gods.

When Elijah marched into Ahab's court and announced that there was going to be a serious drought in Israel, we can be sure that Ahab told Jezebel exactly what Elijah had prophesied. Together, they probably had a good laugh and then forgot all about it. But when Israel's water supply began drying up, you can be sure Ahab began to get nervous. It doesn't take long for "complaining people" to get their king's attention. And God definitely got everyone's attention when the productive and fruitful valleys in Israel began to turn into dust bowls.

An "All-Points Alert"

Ahab focused his frustration on God's prophet just like his pagan counterpart—the pharaoh in Egypt—had done years before. Then it was Moses; now, it's Elijah! Rather than turning from his sins and leading Israel to forsake their idols and to worship Jehovah, Ahab put out an all-points alert to try and bring this troublemaker into custody.

Ahab's actions reveal the extent to which he had forsaken the God of his forefathers. Either he did not realize what he was doing in trying to capture Elijah, or he simply refused to believe what he knew to be true. To wage war on Elijah was to wage war on God Himself. Ahab did not accept the fact that for him—and the people of Israel—this was definitely a no-win situation.

A Direct Word from God

We're not told how soon Ahab's insecurity turned to anger and aggressive actions against Elijah. But when it happened, God was there to protect His servant. It was *then* that "the word of the LORD came to Elijah" (1 Kings 17:2). This time God's message was very specific: "Leave here, turn eastward and hide in the ravine of Kerith, east of the Jordan" (v. 3).

There's no way to determine the exact location of this "hiding place." We can only agree on one thing: It could have been one of many places, since there were numerous ravines in this general area. Apparently this is why it was a safe place for Elijah. Ahab's men could look for days and never find him.

Cool Water and Dirty Birds

God not only provided Elijah with a hiding place, but also took care of his material needs. Since Elijah, too, was a victim of the very drought he had asked God to bring on Israel, God led him to a place where he could drink life-sustaining water from a brook. But in addition to this *natural* provision, the Lord supernaturally provided Elijah with food. "I have ordered the ravens to feed you there," God said (v. 4).

In God's sight, the ravens were "unclean" birds (see Lev. 11:13–15; Deut. 14:11–14). Yet He used them to meet Elijah's needs. What a reminder that the Lord can use even unclean vessels to accomplish His tasks! If Elijah began to doubt his worthiness to be involved in such a dramatic plan— which he would certainly be tempted to do—the ravens would remind him regularly that God can use a man who feels fearful, lonely and unequal to the task.

"I'm in Control!"

In the midst of his plight, Elijah was learning that God had not forsaken him. Remember that he was a "man just like us" and, like us, he certainly would have wondered if God had forsaken him. Think for a moment what it would have been like sitting all alone day after day and week after week in a barren desert ravine!

God was reassuring Elijah that He was still in control. The prophet Isaiah once wrote that God could *"command* the clouds" and they would not yield rain (Isa. 5:6). This is what the Lord had done in response to Elijah's prayer. But God was now working another miracle. There in the wilderness—hiding from Ahab—God was showing His servant He could *command the ravens* to feed him both morning and evening. Daily, when the sun arose and when it set in the evening, the ravens served as a constant reminder that God was still in control of nature.

A Daily Touch with Life

Why didn't God provide Elijah with manna as He had done for the children of Israel years before as they wandered in the wilderness? Could it be that God was being sensitive to Elijah's loneliness? Rather than leaving him alone in a wilderness setting—surrounded with trees, bushes, and shrubs that were beginning to reflect a look of death—God provided a daily touch with life. How Elijah must have looked forward to seeing those ravens arrive each morning and evening!

God could have provided Elijah with either bread or meat. He certainly could have survived on one or the other. But God provided Elijah with both—a balanced diet. God added "something extra" to encourage Elijah.

Only God knows, of course, the real reasons He had for sending ravens to feed Elijah. It seems apparent, however, that He wanted to meet Elijah's needs, not only physically but psychologically and spiritually as well. It's a marvelous reminder that God cares about His children—particularly those who are serving Him in special ways and who need care and encouragement.

Getting Ready

When God uses people in special ways to accomplish His purposes in this world, He prepares them well. Oftentimes this kind of learning involves experiences that generate feelings of isolation, rejection, and loneliness. But always, this preparation is tailored and designed just for the person involved. God knows in exact detail what we need to get ready to face the challenges that lie before us!

The Desert Experience

This was true of Moses! He spent forty years in isolation on the backside of the desert after his prominent forty years in Egypt. Though he did not realize it at the time, God was preparing him for the greatest task any human being would ever face—the challenge of leading the children of Israel out of Egypt.

Years in Prison

Joseph spent a number of years in an Egyptian prison before he was promoted to be prime minister. Without those difficult and lonely prison experiences and the rejection he felt, Joseph would never have been ready for the task God designed for him.

Alone in Arabia

The apostle Paul—following his conversion to Christ—spent three lonely years in Arabia. While he was there, God was preparing him to become the greatest missionary who ever lived.

Prior to his conversion, Paul was a prominent Pharisee. He had a huge ego. By his own confession, he was arrogant and insensitive to others' needs (see Phil. 3:4–6). Without his "wilderness experience," Paul would never have been ready to be the man God wanted to use in a special way to reach Gentiles for Christ.

Years of Obscurity

Even our Lord Jesus Christ, the Son of God and Savior of the world, spent thirty years in obscurity before entering a public ministry. His forty days in the wilderness was a final touch to prepare Him to face the lonely road which lay ahead and which resulted in the cross.

It should not surprise us, then, that God was doing something special in Elijah's life in preparing him for what was yet to come. And in future chapters, we'll see why Elijah needed this unusual preparation.

Becoming God's Man Today

Principles to Live By

Principle 1. God does not normally speak to us today as He did in biblical days.

Every Christian can identify in a special way with Elijah. James tells us why. Though he was a great prophet of God, he was still "a man just like us." However, we must be careful when we make life applications.

We can learn powerful lessons from this Old Testament prophet. However, we must not generalize from Elijah's experience to our own in every particular. For example, God often spoke *directly* to Elijah. That's why he's identified as an Old Testament *prophet.* He often became God's divine "mouthpiece" to Israel.

How God Speaks Today

There are some very sincere people who believe that God communicates with them today just like He did with Elijah. God could, of course, for He can do anything He wants to do; He's not limited by time or space. Mostly, however, He has not chosen to speak in this way. Rather, once He spoke *through* His apostles and prophets and gave us the holy Scriptures, He now uses His revealed Word to communicate with us. Generally speaking, the Scriptures give us everything we need to know to be able to determine His will for our lives.

An Experience Worth Listening To

One day a lady approached me regarding her husband. He was not a Christian and wanted nothing to do with her spiritual convictions, her church, or her Lord. He had secured an attorney and was trying to have her evicted from the home. Previously, she had also secured an attorney, but had released him from the case because she believed God had "told her" that her husband was going to become a Christian, that he was going to accept her spiritual convictions, and that he was going to go with her and her family to serve as missionaries on the foreign mission field. But things didn't seem to be working out the way she believed God had "told her" it would happen.

Let me make it perfectly clear that this lady was not mentally or emotionally ill. She was not "hearing voices." Rather, she was simply acting on what she had been taught—that God speaks to Christians today just as He did to Elijah. As I listened carefully to her story, I concluded that she had taken an experience like Elijah's and had tried to duplicate it in her own—which had resulted in a subjective, psychological experience.

"I'm not sure it was God speaking to you," I told her as sensitively as I could.

"You aren't?" she asked. "Was it Satan then?" reflecting another confused view regarding supernatural communications.

"No, I don't believe it was Satan," I replied.

"Was it just me?" she asked.

"Yes," I responded. "I believe it was probably just you—your deep desire to see your husband come to Christ, your hope for the future!"

In this instance, this woman seemed to be "speaking to herself," even though she sincerely believed it was God speaking to her through her mind. Her deep desires had become internal verbal signals.

Later in our conversation, the same woman indicated that she also believed that God had given her a similar message through some verses of Scripture she had discovered in the Book of Acts. Wasn't this a confirmation that God had spoken to her in her mind? Again, I sensitively took her to the passage in the Bible and I explained the context. The Holy Spirit showed her immediately that she had been misusing the Word of God.

Can you see how dangerous it can be either to believe that God is speaking *directly* through our mental and psychological apparatus, or to believe that God is speaking through Scripture that has been taken out of context? There are people who very sincerely walk out of God's will because they listen to these "voices" from within. The voice Elijah heard was not from within. It was external. It was *from God.*

Principle 2. God has made promises in His Word that are always true, no matter when or where we live.

When we study the whole of Scripture, it's very clear that God has promised to be with us at all times. However, He has never promised that He will *always deliver us* from problems, difficulties, or even death. But He has promised to sustain us and never to leave our side.

God May or God May Not

Even Shadrach, Meshach, and Abednego recognized this distinction. They made it clear to King Nebuchadnezzar that the God they served *was* able to protect them from death— even a fiery furnace. In this case, God did. But before they even entered the furnace, they also knew He might not! And they also made that clear to the king—that if God chose to take them to heaven, they would still not serve false gods (see Dan. 3:17–18).

"The Lord Will Rescue Me"

The apostle Paul also understood this very important distinction. Before he died, probably executed by the evil Roman emperor, Nero, he wrote these words to Timothy:

> At my first defense, no one came to my support, but everyone deserted me. May it not be held against them. But the Lord stood at my side and gave me strength, so that through me the message might be fully proclaimed and all the Gentiles might hear it. And I was delivered from the lion's mouth. The Lord

will rescue me from every evil attack and will bring me safely to his heavenly kingdom. To Him be glory for ever and ever. Amen. (2 Tim. 4:16–18)

By Life or by Death

Paul knew that God would never forsake him—whether he lived or died. He was confident that he could face his persecutors triumphantly. His deliverance would come—either to remain on this earth to fulfill God's will or to be set free from his earthly body and enjoy the splendors of heaven.

Paul knew that he would be free either way. He sensed God's divine protection. This is what he meant when he wrote to the Philippians from a Roman prison: "I eagerly expect and hope that I will in no way be ashamed, but will have sufficient courage so that now as always Christ will be exalted in my body, whether by life or by death. For to me, to live is Christ and to die is gain" (Phil. 1:20–21).

The Scriptures teach that this kind of protection is *always* available to a believer—no matter when we live or where we live. Jesus Christ will never leave us or forsake us. Christians who have faced this kind of persecution throughout the centuries have demonstrated in dramatic ways that this is true. Some have lived to talk about it.

Martyred in China

Some have died for their faith like John and Betty Stam who were martyred for the cause of Christ when the communists took over in China in the 1930s. They literally gave their lives for Jesus Christ. When Will Houghton, then president of Moody Bible Institute, heard about this human tragedy, he penned the following words to give a proper Christian perspective:

> So this is life, this world with all its pleasures,
> Struggles and tears, a smile, a frown, a sigh,
> Friendship so true, and love of kin and neighbor?
> Sometimes 'tis hard to live—always, to die!

The world moves on, so rapidly the living
The forms of those who disappear replace,
And each one dreams that he will be enduring—
How soon that one becomes the missing face!

In life or death—and life is surely flying,
The crib and coffin carved from the self-same tree.
In life or death—and death so soon is coming—
Escape I cannot, there's no place to flee—
But Thou, O God, hast life that is eternal;
That life is mine, a gift thro' Thy dear Son.
Help me to feel its flush and pulse supernal,
Assurance of the morn when life is done.

Help me to know the value of these hours,
Help me the folly of all waste to see;
Help me to trust the Christ who bore my sorrows,
And thus to yield for life or death to Thee.
In all my days be glorified, Lord Jesus,
In all my ways guide me with Thine own eye;
Just when and as Thou wilt, use me, Lord Jesus,
And then for me 'tis Christ, to live or die.[1]

Delivered from Death in Uganda

Kefa Sempangi founded and pastored the 14,000-member Redeemed Church of Uganda, which became a target of Idi Amin's intense persecution in 1973. Thousands of people throughout the country were exterminated by Amin's Nubian assassins. However, God chose to miraculously deliver Kefa and his family from death. Kefa describes one of those moments in his book, *A Distant Grief.* It was Easter Sunday, and Kefa had preached most of the day to thousands who had gathered from miles around. At the end of the day, as the sun was going down, he closed the service. And then it happened!

> I greeted several more friends and then left for the vestry to change my clothes, hoping to have a few minutes alone in prayer. I had to push my way through the crowd and when I

finally arrived at the house, I was exhausted. I was too tired to notice the men behind me until they had closed the door.

There were five of them. They stood between me and the door, pointing their rifles at my face. Their own faces were scarred with the distinctive tribal cuttings of the Kakwa tribe. They were dressed casually in flowered shirts and bell-bottom pants, and wore sunglasses. Although I had never seen any of them before, I recognized them immediately. They were the secret police of the State Research Bureau—Amin's Nubian assassins.

For a long moment no one said anything. Then the tallest man, obviously the leader, spoke. "We are going to kill you," he said. "If you have something to say, say it before you die." He spoke quietly but his face was twisted with hatred.

I could only stare at him. For a sickening moment I felt the full weight of his rage. We had never met before, but his deepest desire was to tear me to pieces. My mouth felt heavy and my limbs began to shake. Everything left my control. They will not need to kill me, I thought to myself. I am just going to fall over. I am going to fall over dead and I will never see my family again. I thought of Penina home alone with Damali. What would happen to them when I was gone?

From far away I heard a voice, and I was astonished to realize it was my own. "I do not need to plead my own cause," I heard myself saying. "I am a dead man already. My life is dead and hidden in Christ. It is your lives that are in danger, you are dead in your sins. I will pray to God that after you have killed me, He will spare you from eternal destruction."

The tall one took a step towards me and then stopped. In an instant, his face was changed. His hatred had turned to curiosity. He lowered his gun and motioned to the others to do the same. They stared at him in amazement but they took their guns from my face.

Then the tall one spoke again. "Will you pray for us now?" he asked.

I thought my ears were playing a trick. I looked at him and then at the others. My mind was completely paralyzed. The tall one repeated his question more loudly, and I could see that he was becoming impatient.

"Yes, I will pray for you," I answered. My voice sounded bolder even to myself. "I will pray to the Father in heaven. Please bow your heads and close your eyes."

The tall one motioned to the others again, and together the five of them lowered their heads. I bowed my own head, but I kept my eyes open. The Nubian's request seemed to me a strange trick. Any minute, I thought to myself, my life will end. I did not want to die with my eyes closed.

"Father in heaven," I prayed, "You who have forgiven men in the past; forgive these men also. Do not let them perish in their sins but bring them unto Yourself."

It was a simple prayer, prayed in deep fear. But God looked beyond my fears and when I lifted my head, the men standing in front of me were not the same men who had followed me into the vestry. Something had changed in their faces.

It was the tall one who spoke first. His voice was bold but there was no contempt in his words. "You have helped us," he said, "and we will help you. We will speak to the rest of our company and they will leave you alone. Do not fear for your life. It is in our hands and you will be protected."

I was too astonished to reply. The tall one only motioned for the others to leave. He himself stepped to the doorway and then he turned to speak one last time. "I saw widows and orphans in the congregation," he said. "I saw them singing and giving praise. Why are they happy when death is so near?"

It was still difficult to speak but I answered him. "Because they are loved by God. He has given them life, and will give life to those they loved, because they died in Him."

His question seemed strange to me, but he did not stay to explain. He only shook his head in perplexity and walked out the door."[2]

Becoming a Man of the Word

One of the great lessons we can learn from this event in Elijah's life is to become a careful student of the Scriptures.

➤ God *does* speak today—but He speaks primarily through the Scriptures. We must be careful to understand all of His promises in proper context.

➤ God does deliver us today from various problems and difficulties. However, He may not deliver us "out of" those difficulties. But He will *always* enable us to *endure* them—even if it means boldly giving our lives for Christ.

As you reflect on the principles in this study, ask the Holy Spirit to impress on your heart one lesson you need to apply more effectively in your life. Then write out a specific goal. For example, you may recognize that you take Scripture out of context. Or, you may be relying on subjective experience to determine the will of God.

Set a Goal

With God's help, I will begin immediately to carry out the following goal in my life:

_____

_____

_____

_____

Memorize the Following Scripture

I eagerly expect and hope that I will in no way be ashamed, but will have sufficient courage so that now as always Christ will be exalted in my body, whether by life or by death. For to me, to live is Christ and to die is gain.

PHILIPPIANS 1:20–21

Chapter 3

Experiencing God's Faithfulness
Read 1 Kings 17:7–16

*M*y wife, Elaine, has been a wonderful example to me when it comes to faith and trusting God. During the early years of our marriage, we had an unusual need. There was too much month left after the paycheck had been spent—including what we had given for our monthly tithe, which we had always set aside for the Lord before spending money on other things. We had a newborn baby and we literally didn't have enough money to buy formula.

"Lord, We Need Help!"

Elaine remembers standing at the ironing board one afternoon talking to God about our predicament. "Lord," she said, "we need help! I don't know where to get the money to buy food for our baby." She knew we would run out before I'd get my next paycheck.

Later that afternoon, a mailman delivered an envelope from Sears & Roebuck. Elaine suspected it was a monthly bill, but when she opened the envelope, she found a refund for overpayment. "This can't be," Elaine said to herself. She has always kept meticulous financial records. She was absolutely sure the refund was a mistake.

Would you believe that the check was the exact amount we needed to buy formula? It would have been easy for her to conclude that this was the way the Lord had provided. However, her conscience wouldn't let her cash the check. Rather, she immediately called Sears & Roebuck and informed them that they had made a mistake.

Try as she might, Elaine couldn't convince the girl on the other end of the line that we hadn't overpaid. Rather, the girl convinced her that they couldn't accept it back so she might as well cash the check and spend it.

When Elaine hung up the phone, she then saw this was an unusual answer to her prayer. At just the right moment, God provided the money in a very strange way to buy formula for our baby. Incidentally, Elaine still believes it was their mistake —not ours!

God *does* care about His children. Sometimes we have to wait until the last moment to experience His faithfulness, but He has promised to meet our needs if we put Him first (see Matt. 6:33).

In essence, this is Elijah's life story and experience. After confronting King Ahab, he had already experienced God's faithful care in "the Kerith Ravine." There he drank from a brook and every morning and evening ate bread and meat delivered by ravens. However, he was about to learn more about God's faithfulness.

When the Brook Dried Up

We're not told how long Elijah lived in that secluded ravine. Some believe it was at least a year—maybe longer. As the drought continued, Elijah's anxiety level must have risen as the stream of water slowed to a mere trickle. Eventually, "the brook dried up" altogether (1 Kings 17:7).

All during this period of isolation from the outside world, Elijah never missed a meal. Like clockwork, the ravens arrived every morning and evening with bread and meat. However, at the same time, the water level in the brook was getting lower and lower. I'm sure Elijah remembered how the Lord had brought water out of the rocks for Israel when they traveled through the wilderness. If God had answered Elijah's prayer in withholding the rain, surely He could answer another prayer and provide him with water.

Fading Memories

It's difficult to build our faith on a historical event—especially when it happened years before. It's doubly difficult to trust God when those events happen to other people. It's hard to identify—and our memories also fade!

We must remember again that "Elijah was a man just like us," which means he was subject to the same temptations we all are. Even though our needs are being met in one or several areas, it seems to be the area where our needs are *not* being met that create our greatest frustration and doubt. If I had been Elijah, my need for water would probably tend to overshadow all of my other needs. Watching the flow of water as it got slower and slower would certainly create an element of panic.

Imagine, too, the temptation Elijah must have faced to want to reverse God's judgment. After all, it was his prayers that caused the Lord to shut the windows of heaven, and eventually it would be his prayers that would once again bring rain. His own fears and needs at that moment in his life must have tempted him to speed up the process.

At the Last Moment!

When did God speak to Elijah? It happened just as the brook dried up! It was then—and not before—that "the word of the LORD" came to Elijah, directing him away from Kerith. "Go at once to Zarephath of Sidon and stay there," God said. "I have commanded a widow in that place to supply you with food" (17:8–9).

God's command to "go at once" underscores how urgent the situation had become. Elijah, of course, wasted no time in responding to God's command. He met the widow—just as God said he would. She was gathering sticks at the gate of the city.

The Widow at Zarephath

Why a Poor Widow?

It's not an accident that God chose a widow to meet Elijah's needs—a woman who had only enough food for a final meal. Why did God choose this lonely, destitute person?

God is concerned when we are in need. God chose this widow because she and her son were running out of food. When Elijah asked her for a drink of water and some bread, she replied, "I don't have any bread—only a handful of flour in a jar and a little oil in a jug. I am gathering a few sticks to take home and make a meal for myself and my son, that we may eat it—and die" (v. 12).

The widow's comment was sincere. It was not just feeling sorry for herself. She was desperate! Fear was written all over her face. That's why Elijah responded, "Don't be afraid" (v. 13). For days, she must have cautiously limited the intake of food for both her son and herself—which was reflected not only in her fear and anxiety but what must have been a frail body that lacked nourishment.

Few of us have ever experienced being down to our last meal for our family, with no way to obtain more food. And certainly few of us have ever been in a situation where we've been asked to give what little we have left to someone else. Simply facing the prospect of starvation over a lengthy period of time would be enough to demoralize a human being. And now Elijah was asking her to share her final morsel of food with him! No wonder her face was filled with fear and anxiety.

I believe God sent Elijah to this poor widow because she was a person who was in deep need physically and spiritually. The Lord knew her food supply was almost gone. Perhaps she had been praying and asking God for help.

God responds to people who are seeking to know Him, no matter what their status in life. This poor widow lived in Sidon, a Gentile community. Ironically, it was the same area in which Jezebel lived before she married Ahab. She was evidently seeking the real truth about God and beautifully illustrates God's concern for *all people* everywhere.

Wherever people are seeking God, He is ready to reveal His mercy. It doesn't matter who they are or what their background or resources. The Lord honors faith—just as He did in the life of another Gentile woman many years later who lived in the very same geographical area as this widow at Zarephath. This woman came to Jesus one day, asking that He might heal her daughter who was demon possessed. Jesus did not respond immediately and the disciples picked up on His silence and tried to send her away. Prejudice was written all over their faces.

In time, however, Jesus did respond and told her that He had been "sent only to the lost sheep of Israel" (Matt. 15:24). At this moment, the disciples must have swollen with arrogance and pride. But rather than leaving—as the disciples tried to get her to do—she humbled herself and knelt before Jesus, pleading for mercy and help.

Jesus once again spoke to her, using words that seem out of character. "It is not right to take the children's bread and toss it to their dogs" (v. 26). Again, the disciples must have nodded their heads in agreement and again, attempted to get her to leave the scene.

It may appear that Jesus was speaking only to the woman; however, He was actually speaking more directly to His disciples. Knowing their terrible prejudice toward Gentiles, Jesus was probably verbalizing what they were thinking. Jesus was achieving two goals at the same time. First, He was testing the faith of this Gentile woman. But even more importantly, He was teaching His disciples a powerful lesson.

The woman's final response set the stage for Jesus to drive home a great spiritual truth into the hearts of His disciples.

"Yes, Lord," she replied, "but even the dogs eat the crumbs that fall from their masters' table" (v. 27).

If the disciples had been listening carefully and evaluating their own hearts, these words alone from the Gentile woman are a powerful message. Jesus was waiting for this moment. He put the finishing touches on what He was trying to accomplish in the lives of the disciples as well as in the life of the woman. "Woman," He responded, "you have great faith! Your request is granted." At that very moment, He healed her daughter (v. 28).

Jesus had just taught two lessons simultaneously: One to a Gentile woman who needed to develop her faith. The other lesson—and perhaps the most important one—was what He taught the disciples who desperately needed to know that some Gentiles actually had more faith than they did. In their prejudice, they were blinded to their own self-righteousness.

Elijah's encounter with the widow of Zarephath is an Old Testament prelude to this New Testament story. Elijah was sent to a Gentile woman for help. She was in deep need, and since she was seeking to know God, the Lord not only was going to use Elijah to meet a deep need in her own life, but also to use this event to meet a special need in Elijah's life.

One of the major lessons God is teaching us in both of these stories is that He can minister in a special way to a variety of people with various needs with a single event. And this leads us to another reason God chose this widow in this Old Testament setting.

God was reassuring Elijah of His continual presence and power. Elijah had a gigantic task ahead of him and he needed reassurance that God was still in control. For at least a year, the Lord had commanded the ravens to feed him. And now God prepared a widow lady to demonstrate His continued presence and power.

The message is clear! God does not need great and mighty subjects to be His ministers. If He can use "unclean birds" as well as a poor Gentile widow, He can certainly use anything and anyone! Elijah needed that continual reassurance.

God was also teaching Elijah to continue to rely upon Him. If God had sent Elijah to someone who had a great supply of food, he may have been tempted to stop praying and trusting God. How quickly that happens when we have no serious need.

Elijah evidently knew exactly what God was about to do. His faith was strong. He knew that God was going to take care of *all of them*—the widow, her son, and himself. "Go home," he said, "and do as you have said. But first make a small cake of bread for me from what you have and bring it to me, and then make something for yourself and your son. For this is what the LORD, the God of Israel, says: 'The jar of flour will not be used up and the jug of oil will not run dry until the day the LORD gives rain on the land'" (1 Kings 17:13–14).

God honored this woman's faith and obedience—just as Jesus would do many years later. She responded to Elijah's reassurance. Sure enough, "there was food every day for Elijah and for the woman and her family. For the jar of flour was not used up and the jug of oil did not run dry, in keeping with the word of the LORD spoken by Elijah" (vv. 15–16).

Note that God supplied "food every day." There was never more or less than they needed. In actuality, this was a more important lesson for Elijah than for the woman. You see, all during this period of waiting, God kept reassuring Elijah of His power and protection. The ravens appeared with food every morning and evening, which was a constant reminder of God's faithfulness. And now the jar and jug were never empty. Elijah needed this constant reminder to prepare him for the task that still lay ahead of him.

The Lord could have miraculously provided Elijah and his newfound friends with a huge barrel of flour and a large keg of oil. If He had, there would have been no need to keep trusting God day by day. Elijah, like all of us, needed to learn to trust God constantly.

Becoming God's Man Today

Principles to Live By

Principle 1. God is concerned about all people.

It doesn't matter who you are, your age, your sex, your marital status, your economic situation, or your ethnic background. You can be Jew or Gentile, black or white, rich or poor. God loves you! Elijah's experience with the widow of Zarephath illustrates this point beautifully.

We must remember that the gospel is for all people. Though Jesus was a Jew and came to His own people first, He did so to launch a mission to people everywhere. This is why He said to His disciples, "You will be my witnesses in Jerusalem, and in all Judea and Samaria, and to the ends of the earth" (Acts 1:8). The greatest truth in all of Scripture is what Jesus said one day to Nicodemus—"For God so loved the world that he gave his one and only Son, that whoever believes in him shall not perish but have eternal life" (John 3:16).

Principle 2. God honors those who put others first.

Consider Paul's word to the Philippians: "Do nothing out of selfish ambition or vain conceit, but in humility consider others better than yourselves. Each of you should look not only to your own interests, but also the interests of others" (Phil. 2:3–4).

Think for a moment how difficult it must have been for the widow woman to take all that she had to eat and share it with Elijah first. That would be difficult for anyone of us.

Many years later, Jesus once again illustrated this principle with another poor widow. One day He was watching people in the temple as they filed by to put their gifts in a special offering box. Using today's language, one person put in $10, another $100, and someone else $1,000. But, we read that "He also saw a poor widow put in two very small copper coins."

Jesus was deeply moved and used this event as a teaching point. "I tell you the truth," He said, "this poor widow has put in more than all the others. All these people gave their gifts out of their wealth; but she out of her poverty put in all she had to live on" (Luke 21:1–4).

Was Jesus saying that poor people should give all they have? Certainly not! The message was for those who had more than she did. He was saying that she gave *more* than all of them. If those who gave large amounts were to give sacrificially, they would have to give far more of what they had left over. Furthermore, He was also dealing with their pride and arrogance and their self-righteousness.

At one point in my ministry, I had the opportunity to lead a group of laymen in my church through a study of everything the Bible has to say about material possessions. We were amazed at what we discovered. In fact, God says more about how we use our material possessions than any subject other than Himself.[1]

Why does God emphasize our material possessions so frequently? Dr. Charles Ryrie answers this question very specifically in his book, *Balancing the Christian Life:*

> To be sure, a vital spiritual life is related to fellowship with the Lord in His word and prayer and to service for the Lord in His work. But our love for God may be proved by something that is a major part of everyone's life, and that is our use of money. How we use our money demonstrates the reality of our love for God. In some ways it proves our love more conclusively than depth of knowledge, length of prayers or prominence of service. These things can be feigned, but the use of our possessions shows us up for what we actually are.[2]

Principle 3. God delights in taking what we have— our talents, our time, our material resources— and multiplying their effectiveness.

For the widow at Zarephath, it was a "jar of meal" and a "jug of oil." There was always enough left over for every day. This, of course, was a dramatic miracle. It had to be if she and her son— and Elijah—were going to survive.

"But, Will God Do This for Me?"

To answer this question, we must understand that God can do anything He desires. His power is unlimited; He is the unchangeable God. But, we must also understand that He follows His own rules. For example, the supernatural provision He made for the widow, her son, and Elijah continued only until it began to rain again (see 1 Kings 17:14). When the natural means were available (in this case, a conducive climate for producing food), God expected people to provide for themselves from the natural resources that He had already provided.

There are times in all of our lives when we must turn to God for supernatural help. We need His divine intervention. When we trust Him day by day and, at the same time, do everything we can with the resources that He has given us, and yet we cannot meet our needs, God is able and willing to go beyond our natural capabilities. God can and will do this, just as He did it in this Old Testament story.

A Miracle in South Africa

I remember talking to a man from India who was serving as a missionary to his own people in South Africa. On one occasion, they had no food in the house. In fact, they'd given away what they had to meet someone else's need. However, they had a garden—but the vegetables were just breaking through the ground. It would be weeks before they could count on these plants for food. However, after committing their need for food to the Lord, John awakened the next morning to discover that some of the vegetable plants had matured overnight! A miracle? I believe so. God can still do for people today what He did for the widow at Zarephath.

Balance Is the Key

We see an incredible balance in the story of the rebuilding of the walls of Jerusalem under the leadership of Nehemiah. These people worked hard, doing everything they could to rebuild the walls. They planned, they organized, and at times they worked around the clock. But there were also times when they had to face the fact that they needed God's supernatural intervention. Though they had been praying and trusting God all along, they needed to stop and say, "Lord, without your miraculous help, we can't go on. We cannot succeed." God again and again miraculously met their needs.

Principle 4. At times the Lord keeps us on the edge of uncertainty to develop our faith in Him.

What if the Lord had led Elijah from the ravine of Kerith to a fruitful plantation flowing with milk and honey? I'm certain that Elijah would have enjoyed it. However, I'm convinced that Elijah would have followed his human tendency—a tendency in us all—to get sidetracked from the mission God had for him. Remember that he was "a man just like us." You see, God in His omniscience knew that the mission that lay ahead of Elijah was going to call for spiritual faith and emotional energy far beyond anything that he'd ever experienced before.

When everything is going smoothly, when we have all we need, when the road is clear and smooth before us, we tend to overrely on our wisdom, our abilities, and our own energy. I'm convinced that God often provides opportunities for us to grow in our faith in order to be even more effective in our work for Him.

Taking Successes for Granted

The tendency to take our successes for granted can be illustrated at even a very human level. I used to have long conversations with Dave Manders, all-pro center for the Dallas Cowboys in the glory days when Tom Landry coached this dynamic group of guys. Dave was convinced that Coach Landry purposely put them in a slump mid-season to keep them from becoming overconfident and peaking too soon. Did it work? You be the judge, since they went all the way to the Super Bowl on several occasions. You see, Tom Landry understood how easily we can lose focus when we're winning, when the road seems too smooth, when we feel we're a team that can't be beat!

The same principle applies in our spiritual lives. This is particularly true for those of us who live in a "land flowing with milk and honey." Opportunities are everywhere! Why pray? Why trust God? Why rely on Him when we can make our way in life, even as Christians?

Let's Meet Kefa Once Again

When I read the story told by Kefa Sempangi, I realized as never before the effects of culture on all of us. After he and his wife and family were miraculously delivered from certain death in Uganda, they came to the United States to study. Just a few months after he came to America, he noticed a change that was taking place in his life. Here are his own words:

> Our first semester passed quickly. Penina gave birth to our son, Dawudi Babumba. In the fall I returned to my studies. It was then, in my second year, that I noticed the change that had come into my life. In Uganda, Penina and I read the Bible for hope and life. We read to hear God's promises, to hear His commands and obey them. There had been no time for argument, no time for religious discrepancies or doubts.

> Now, in the security of a new life and with the reality of death fading from my mind, I found myself reading Scripture to analyze texts and to speculate about meaning. I came to enjoy abstract discussions with my fellow students and, while these discussions were intellectually refreshing, it wasn't long before our fellowship revolved around ideas rather than the work of God in our lives. It was not the blood of Christ that gave us unity, but our agreement on doctrinal issues. We came together not for confession and forgiveness but for debate.

> The biggest change came to my prayer life. In Uganda I had prayed with a deep sense of urgency. I refused to leave my knees until I was certain I had been in the presence of the resurrected

Christ. It was not just the gift I needed. I needed to see the Giver. I needed to know that the God of orphans and widows, the God of the helpless, heard my prayers. Now, after a year in Philadelphia, the urgency was gone. When I prayed publicly I was more concerned to be theologically correct than to be in God's presence. Even in private my prayers were no longer the helpless cries of a child. They were spiritual tranquilizers, thoughts that made no contact with anything outside themselves. More and more I found myself coming to God with vague requests for gifts I did not expect.

One night I said my prayers in a routine fashion and was about to rise from my knees when I heard the convicting voice of the Holy Spirit.

"Kefa, who were you praying for? What is it you wanted? I used to hear the names of children in your prayers, the names of friends and relatives. . . . Now you pray for 'the orphans,' for 'the church' and your 'fellow-refugees.' Which refugees, Kefa? Which believers? Which orphans? Who are these people and what is it you want for them?"

It was a sharp rebuke. As I fell again to my knees and asked forgiveness for my sin of unbelief, I knew that it was not just my prayers that had suffered. It was not just a bad memory that had caused names to vanish from my mind and turned those closest to me into abstractions. God Himself had become a distant figure. He had become a subject of debate, an abstract category. I no longer prayed to Him as a living Father, but as an impersonal being who did not mind my inattention and unbelief.

From that night on, my prayers became specific. I prayed for real people, with real needs. And it was not long before, once again, these needs became the means by which I came face to face with the living God.[3]

Don't Misunderstand!

God does not want us to live in a constant state of tension. Even Elijah couldn't handle that kind of experience. God also wants us to enjoy the good things of life. We all need relief from pressures. Even Jesus needed that as well as His disciples. That's why He said one day, "Come with me by yourselves to a quiet place and get some rest" (Mark 6:31).

Remember, too, the words Paul wrote to the Philippians: "I know what it is to be in need, and I know what it is to have plenty. I have learned the secret of being content in any and every situation, whether well fed or hungry, whether living in plenty or in want." And then Paul gave us a grand conclusion —"I can do everything through him who gives me strength" (Phil. 4:12–13).

Becoming a Man of Faith

As you evaluate the principles in this chapter, pray and ask the Holy Spirit to impress on your heart one lesson you need to apply more effectively in order to become a man of faith. Then write out a specific goal. For example, you may be having difficulty believing that God can take what you have and multiply it for His glory.

Ask Yourself These Questions

1. Do I really believe that God cares for me? (He does, of course!) Do I accept that fact? Do I believe it?

2. To what extent am I thinking of others' needs before I think of my own? How is this reflected in my stewardship of time, my material resources, and my abilities?

3. Do I believe God can take what I have and multiply it? What evidence do I have that I believe this?

4. How strong is my faith? How much do I really rely upon God? Is it possible that some of my uncertainties at the present time are ordered by the Lord to develop my spiritual life? Am I resisting God or am I submitting to Him in order to learn more about His plan for my life?

Set a Goal

With God's help, I will begin immediately to carry out the following goal in my life:

_____

_____

_____

_____

Memorize the Following Scripture

I know what it is to be in need, and I know what it is to have plenty. I have learned the secret of being content in any and every situation, whether well fed or hungry, whether living in plenty or in want. I can do everything through him who gives me strength.

PHILIPPIANS 4:12–13

Chapter 4

Learning the Power of Prayer
Read 1 Kings 17:17–24

*H*ave you ever stopped to reflect on the times you've really prayed? I mean, *really* prayed! Of course, we can all remember the times we talked to God routinely:

➤ "Lord, thank you for this food!"

➤ "Father, please watch over us as we begin this trip as a family."

➤ "Dear Lord, please open our hearts and minds as we begin this Bible study."

➤ "Dear Jesus, watch over us as we lie down to rest."

Crisis Praying

Remember the times you've cried out to God intently, fervently, with deep emotion? If you're like I am, this happens when you've faced a crisis, a problem, a challenge—something in your life that you can't solve in your own strength or even with the wisdom God gave you once before. It is then we realize that we really need God's help.

Unfortunately, we don't really learn to pray until we face circumstances that seem to be beyond our control. Don't misunderstand! God is sympathetic to this tendency in our lives. Furthermore, He realizes that we can't live life in the context of crises that keep us on the edge of insanity. But He also knows that there will be times in our lives when prayer must become a very important focus so that He can use us to achieve His purposes in this world.

Elijah's Greatest Prayer Challenge

God was teaching Elijah an important lesson—a lesson on prayer. Elijah *was* a man of prayer. He'd already proved that. As James reminds us, Elijah "*prayed earnestly* that it would not rain; and it *did not rain* on the land for three and a half years" (James 5:17). However, his greatest opportunity to trust God in prayer still lay ahead when he faced the prophets of Baal on Mount Carmel. To prepare Elijah for this great prayer challenge, God orchestrated another opportunity for him to grow in his prayer life—and in his faith, a spiritual quality that is always associated with effective prayer.

God's plan was right on schedule. To this point, Elijah had passed every test—and God had met his every need. When he feared for his life, God told him where to hide. When there was no food, God used the ravens to feed him. When the brook dried up, God sent him to a widow in Sidon. And when Elijah discovered that this poor woman had no food left to share, God provided enough oil and meal to care for them all. As this man of God faced what appeared to be one insurmountable obstacle after another, Elijah cleared every hurdle and God met his needs.

Did Elijah ever doubt? I'm sure he did! After all, he "was a man just like us." At times, he must have wondered about his sanity when he took on the king of Israel in the name of his God. He must have gone through periods of deep doubt wondering whether God was still in control. But even if Elijah worried, God was faithful. In every instance, he didn't know how and when God was going to take care of him, but the

Lord never failed him—even in the final moments when everything seemed to be falling apart.

Illness Strikes

God designed another crisis to prepare Elijah to encounter Ahab and his false prophets face to face. It was one of the greatest tests he had faced thus far (see 1 Kings 17:17–18).

Several months after Elijah came to live with the widow, her son "became ill." Although the widow's oil jug and her meal jar never ran empty, it didn't keep sickness from invading her life.

It was not a sudden attack that left her son near death. Rather, the boy's health deteriorated over a period of time. He grew "worse and worse, and finally stopped breathing" (1 Kings 17:17). As Elijah watched his little friend deteriorate, I'm sure he must have thought long and hard about the brook in the Kerith Ravine. It too "died a slow death."

Reading between the Lines

Though this tragic event is very succinctly described, there's room for a lot of realistic speculation. When the boy finally "stopped breathing," the widow poured out her deep feelings of anxiety and distress. "What do you have against me, man of God? Did you come to remind me of my sin and kill my son?" (v. 18)

Imagine what was happening. For days—or perhaps weeks—the boy's illness worsened. The first day or two meant little. After all, the oil and meal were always there! All of us have faced periods of illness that come and go.

As the days passed by, however, everyone came to realize that this was no ordinary illness. The boy was not recovering. His mother's casual concern turned to intense fear—and penetrating introspection. In times like these, it's natural to begin to ask the question, "Why?" Human tragedy is always sobering —especially when it involves death.

Predictable Reactions

Like all of us, the widow looked for a reason for what was happening and her thoughts turned inward. She had come to know Elijah well. He was no ordinary man. He was very different from other men she had known. Her pagan friends were licentious and sinful. She had probably lived the same sinful lifestyle.

But for several months now, she had lived in the same house with a man who *was* different. Not once had he tried to use her for selfish reasons. And even if she had made herself available, he would have discussed with her the eternal laws of God that had been revealed to Israel at Sinai.

She'd come to know Elijah as a "man of God." And the more she came to know him—what he believed and how he lived, and what his mission in life really was—the more she became aware of her own sins. This is why she cried out to Elijah—"What do you have against me, *man of God?* Did you come to remind me of *my sin* and kill my son?"

Questions, Fears, Confusion

Though limited in her knowledge of Abraham, Isaac, and Jacob, this widow was tempted to do what many of us do when tragedy strikes. Our view of God often leads us to wonder if He is punishing us for some sin, either in our past or in the present. Lingering guilt always creates paranoia.

The widow had not yet learned that God does not hold grudges. Though on rare occasions, the Lord has punished sin with death—as He did in taking David's illegitimate son home to heaven, it's not God's normal way of working. That's definitely true when it comes to our past sins. And even when we are committing sins in the present, God is very long-suffering. Even in David's case, when God's law specifically declared that he should die for taking Uriah's life, God let him live because of his repentant heart. That is indeed a merciful God.

To add to her bewilderment, this widow knew that it did not seem logical for Elijah to save both her and her son from starvation, only to turn around and take this precious gift of life away from her. No matter what her sin, it didn't make sense. From this vantage point, we can certainly understand this widow's questions, her fears, and her confusion.

Elijah, Too, Was Perplexed

Elijah had come to know this little family well. After a year of painful loneliness in the ravine of Kerith, imagine how refreshing it was to once again spend his days with people. He was deeply troubled when he saw the boy dying—a child he had come to love. To hear this widow's agonizing questions only intensified his own grief.

Again, we must remind ourselves that Elijah was "a man just like us." Even though he was a prophet of God, he was not exempt from all of the painful emotions that accompany an event like this. There she stood—holding her dead son in her arms—agony written all over her tear-stained face, asking that most difficult question of all—"Why?"

A Vivid Memory

I was only four years old when my sister, Jo Ann—who was just a year younger than I—injured herself on the edge of a low table. While chasing each other around the room—as children do—she jammed into the sharp edge of one of the corners.

She cried for a time, but everything seemed to be all right. My parents never gave it another thought—until several days later when she began to complain of severe pain in her side. Concerned that the problem was growing worse, the local doctor put her in the hospital where they diagnosed her condition as appendicitis. However, when they opened up her little body, they found nothing but a mass of gangrene. In those days there was nothing they could do but sew her back up and hope for a miracle. Just a few days later she died.

Though I was very young, I vividly remember the sadness that permeated our home. Several days after the funeral, I was playing in the kitchen. My mother sat in a chair listening to an old battery-operated radio. She was wiping tears from her eyes. I distinctly remember reaching out and tugging at her hand, trying to get her to do something. I can't recall what I wanted, but I do remember that she pushed me away. I also remember the rejection I felt at that moment.

More importantly, I remember her instant response when she saw the emotional pain in my own face. Reaching out, she pulled me close and apologized. Her words are indelibly impressed on my mind as she expressed them with a tearful voice—"I'm sorry, Gene. I didn't mean to hurt your feelings."

Gently and lovingly, mother explained that she had been listening to a song on the radio. She also told me how the words reminded her of my little sister's death.

There's a reason why I recall her explanation so clearly. There before us on the table was a pair of small white shoes— Jo Ann's shoes. The song she was listening to was entitled "Put My Little Shoes Away." You see, the lyrics of that song told the story of a little girl who was dying and in her own childlike way was telling her mother "to put her little shoes away."

I remember so clearly the tears that day, the words of the song—and somehow in my four-year-old heart I understood and I felt deep compassion for my mother. I distinctly remember trying to comfort her.

Death Always Brings Sadness

When a loved one dies, it always creates heartache. It's very real! There standing before Elijah was a woman with a broken heart. She was holding her little boy in her arms. He had stopped breathing. But what was most painful to Elijah were the questions she was asking! In her emotional pain, she was rejecting him. He had saved her life and now she was accusing him of making her aware of her own sin and then taking the life of her only son in order to punish her.

Elijah had come to this family in the name of God. He had shared his mission and how God had cared for him in the ravine of Kerith. The woman and her son responded to this message and to Elijah's God. They had put their trust first in Elijah and then in the Lord. Now, her son had died. At this moment, Elijah deeply felt her distrust. He had no human explanation for what had happened. He felt God's very name and reputation were at stake. What would people say once they found out what happened? Elijah, too, was confused, distraught, and fearful!

A Prayer We Should Never Forget

"Why God, Why?"

In the midst of his own grief, Elijah asked the woman for her son. He took the boy in his arms, climbed to the upper room where he had been staying, laid him on his own bed and began to pray earnestly. This was no ordinary prayer. Elijah "*cried out* to the LORD!" With deep emotional distress and frustration, he poured his soul out to God—"O LORD my God, have you brought tragedy also upon this widow I am staying with, by causing her son to die?" (1 Kings 17:20).

Elijah "stretched himself out on the boy three times and cried to the LORD, 'O LORD my God, let this boy's life return to him!'" (v. 21). Like Elisha—the man who would eventually succeed him as a prophet of God in Israel—Elijah probably "lay upon the boy, mouth to mouth, eyes to eyes, hands to hands" (2 Kings 4:34).

"Look! He's Alive!"

In His mercy, the Lord heard and answered Elijah's prayer. Life returned to the boy. Imagine the joy that gripped the prophet's soul as he descended the stairs with the boy in his arms and presented him to his mother. "Look," he said, "your son is alive!" (1 Kings 17:23)

When the widow saw it was true, the words that flowed from her mouth spoke volumes. "Now I know," she cried, "that you are a man of God and that the word of the LORD from your mouth is the truth" (v. 24).

The Widow's Accusing Finger

We now know more of the conversation that must have taken place between this woman and Elijah as the boy lay dying. As his condition worsened, the widow began to point an accusing finger at Elijah. She had begun to doubt if Elijah was who he said he was—God's representative. As long as things were going well, she had responded to his message of truth. But when things began to go sour, she began to doubt and to point an accusing finger.

Elijah's Emotional Pain

Those who are in the ministry can probably identify more deeply with Elijah's experience. Almost every pastor has helped someone who, at some point in time, turned and became critical when things did not go well. To be accused of insincerity and of being uncaring when you had truly attempted to reach out to someone is a very painful experience. That's exactly what happened to Elijah. We see his pain expressed in his prayer for the boy. As this woman's spiritual leader, he was also confused. *Was* he the cause of the boy's death? Had the Lord brought tragedy into this family *because of him?* He, too, began to question God's ways.

God Honors Honesty

God not only honored Elijah's persistence in prayer; He also honored his honesty and forthrightness regarding his own doubts, his fears, and his disillusionment—as well as his keen disappointment. The Lord gave the boy new life. But more than that, the widow once again believed and Elijah's joy was restored when he saw his new friends reunited and responding positively to the will of God.

Most important to Elijah, this widow no longer rejected the God he served. This was especially important to Elijah since his own people had turned to false gods. In essence, this was why Elijah was there in the first place—he had taken a stand for the one true God. It's not surprising that he wanted God's name vindicated and honored!

Becoming God's Man Today

Principles to Live By

The most important lesson we can learn from Elijah and the widow at Zarephath revolves around what God was doing to continue to prepare this prophet for even greater struggles against the forces of evil. All along God had been getting Elijah ready for a dramatic and terrifying encounter with King Ahab and the prophets of Baal. What Elijah had just asked God to do for the widow's son was minor compared with what he was going to ask God to do on Mount Carmel.

Principle 1. God prepares us for the big challenges in life by providing us with opportunities to face the smaller challenges victoriously.

Have you ever thought about this principle? I've seen God do this in my own life on a number of occasions. Of course, you must know what to look for or you may not even realize what God is doing.

In some respects, this is a scary thought—at least it is for me. I can look back at some very difficult and painful crises I've considered to be tests of faith. Frankly, in my humanness, I don't want any bigger challenges! But the good news is that God is entrusting us with His work and He doesn't want us to fail. He wants to increase our faith so that bigger challenges seem even smaller when we're adequately prepared.

Principle 2. It is in the midst of situations that are beyond our control that we really learn to pray.

How true this was in Elijah's experience! And how true it is in our own!

In some respects, it's unfortunate that we have to be in a position where our backs are against the wall before we take the privilege of prayer seriously. It appears this has always been true in the history of God's people. Fortunately, God understands our human tendencies. He never turns a deaf ear. Though the outcome may not always be what we might choose, God responds with what is best.

Never hesitate to pray when you're facing a serious problem —even though you may neglect this important spiritual exercise when things seem to be going well. It's natural that we pray more fervently during difficult trials.

Principle 3. God understands our anxieties, our fears, our disappointments, and our disillusionments.

Some people view God as an angry father figure who is ready to pounce on them when they share how they really feel. Not so! If this were true, God would act *before we speak*, for He already knows what we think and feel before we express those thoughts and feelings. Consequently, we might as well tell Him. We should never be fearful of expressing these thoughts and feelings to Him in prayer.

On the other hand, we must always remember that we are talking to God. He cannot be manipulated. There are times, however, that He responds in unusual ways—especially when His reputation and name are at stake.

When God Changes His Mind

Consider the time when Moses was on Mount Sinai receiving the laws of God. With unusual audacity, the children of

Israel shaped and molded a golden calf and bowed down to it. They had even given credit to this idol for bringing them out of Egypt.

Predictably, the Lord was angry with His people. He told Moses to step aside so that He might destroy them. However, Moses—faithful shepherd that he was—reminded the Lord that if He wiped Israel "off the face of the earth," the Egyptians would say "It was with evil intent" that he had "brought them out, to kill them in the mountains" (Exod. 32:12). Moses was reminding God that *His reputation* and *name* were at stake.

We'll never be able to explain how a man like Moses—or any man for that matter—could change God's mind by reminding Him of His reputation. Nevertheless, it's true! We read that "the LORD relented and did not bring on his people the disaster he had threatened" (v. 14).

> *Principle 4. God is particularly responsive to our prayers when we are able to get beyond our own interests and concerns and focus on other people's needs—but especially on His reputation.*

When Elijah faced the crisis with the widow's son, we once again see "a man just like us" appealing to God based on his concern for the Lord's reputation. He definitely had concern for the woman as well. However, he had been identified as a "man of God"—a person who represented the Lord of the universe. From Elijah's point of view, if he was not able to bring this boy back to life, unbelievers would question the very message Elijah was proclaiming.

The widow verified Elijah's concern with her own response when she declared, "Now I know that you are a man of God and that the word of the LORD from your mouth is the truth" (1 Kings 17:24).

A Penetrating Question

When you pray for God's help, are you more concerned about yourself than you are for others? Most of all, are you most concerned about the Lord's reputation? If we focused more on the needs of others and the name of the God we serve, is it possible we'll experience more answers to prayer? I think so!

Don't misunderstand! God wants to meet our personal needs. Paul made this clear when he wrote the Philippians and said, "Do not be anxious about *anything*, but in *everything*, by prayer and petition, with thanksgiving, present your requests to God" (Phil. 4:6). God *is* concerned about our needs as well—whatever they are.

But even so, God's reputation must be first—not ours! His will must be first—not ours! His name must be first—not ours! Put God and others first and experience new power in your prayer life!

A Personal Crisis

I remember very well a time in my own life when I was deeply distressed and burdened about a problem I couldn't solve. I spent a great deal of time in prayer asking God for a solution. However, I finally came to the place where I realized that I was really more concerned with my own reputation than with God's. Looking back, I now understand that I couldn't see that realization until there was nothing I could do.

When I finally submitted and cried out to the Lord with honesty and openness, God responded to my prayers. I remember the moment vividly. "Lord," I said, "it's Your reputation that's important, not mine." From that moment, the "clouds of despair" began to roll away and the "sun began to shine" once more in my life.

This doesn't mean that we shouldn't pray for ourselves—our needs and our concerns. It does mean, however, that we should ask ourselves *why* we're praying for ourselves. There's an ultimate concern that should guide even this kind of personal praying—God's name, God's honor, God's integrity, and His will!

Remember, too, that God can bring honor to Himself in all situations—no matter what the outcome. In Elijah's case, God answered his prayer and restored the boy because it would bring the most honor to His name. We must accept the fact, however, that there are times when God can bring more honor to His name in the midst of human tragedy.

Prayer and Physical Healing

God has never promised to heal all physical infirmities—even though we pray in faith. He has promised, however, to provide grace and strength for every situation—but not always to provide deliverance from death.

The apostle Paul illustrates this in his own life. Though he often healed people with God's power, there came a time in his own life when God did not answer his own prayers for physical healing. He told the Corinthians that he had asked the Lord three times to heal him. In fact, he "pleaded with the Lord to take it away." However, God responded to Paul by reminding him that His grace was sufficient to enable him to handle this infirmity (2 Cor. 12:8–9).

False Guilt

An inaccurate view of God's sovereignty when it comes to healing can lead people to feel inappropriate guilt—often blaming themselves for not having enough faith to be cured through prayer. We must remember that God's will is more important than our will in these matters—and when it comes to physical healing, God has not revealed His specific will.

God does choose to respond to our prayers for healing when it is His will. Furthermore, our faith is foundational when He does choose to answer our prayers. Also, remember that if we do not pray, He may not respond. Prayer does make a difference—whether God responds *with healing* or *with grace* to enable us to bear our burdens.

Becoming a Man of Prayer

As you review the following principles, ask the Holy Spirit to impress on your heart one lesson you need to learn about prayer. Then write out a specific goal. For example, you may be fearful of expressing your anxieties, your fears, your disappointments, and your disillusionments to God. We should not be fearful of expressing these thoughts and feelings to Him in prayer.

> ➤ God prepares us for the big challenges in life by providing us with opportunities to face the smaller challenges victoriously.

> ➤ It's in the midst of situations that are beyond our control that we really learn to pray.

> ➤ God understands our anxieties, our fears, our disappointments, and our disillusionments.

> ➤ God is particularly responsive to our prayers when we are able to get beyond our own interests and concerns and focus on other people's needs, but especially on His reputation.

Set a Goal

With God's help, I will begin immediately to carry out the following goal in my life:

_____

_____

_____

_____

Memorize the Following Scripture

Therefore confess your sins to each other and pray for each other so that you may be healed. The prayer of a righteous man is powerful and effective.

JAMES 5:16

Chapter 5

A Man of Integrity

Read 1 Kings 18:1–16

*O*ne day I was interviewing a friend of mine on my radio program called "Renewal." Mike has occupied a high position in the banking industry for a number of years and has become a strong lay leader in the church I pastor. Mike and I were talking about ethics and how to be a godly man in the business world.

As God would have it, a woman was driving along the road and listening to the program. Her own husband had experienced some severe difficulties in his own secular position in the workplace. He had become disillusioned and confused.

The woman was so impressed with our conversation that she pulled her car over alongside the road, took out a note pad, and wrote down Mike's name and where he worked. When she got home that evening, she shared the information with her husband, Bill, and encouraged him to call Mike.

Bill did! This man and his wife now attend our church and have a whole new perspective on what it really means to be a *Christian* in the world of business.

With God All Things Are Possible

The next event in Elijah's life demonstrates in an unusual way that it's possible to be a man of integrity, even in the midst of a very pagan and hostile environment. It's difficult, but with God's help it's an attainable goal.

Two Years to Prepare

The average American gets a "two-week vacation"—not "two years." However, Elijah's "work schedule" was not average. He spent a lonely year in the Kerith Ravine hiding from Ahab who wanted him captured "dead or alive." And now, he'd just gone through a heart-wrenching experience with the widow of Zarephath. Even though God answered Elijah's agonizing prayer and brought this young boy back to life, it must have left Elijah exhausted. We must never forget that he was "a man just like us." The fact that he was able to perform great miracles doesn't mean he didn't have the same physical and emotional needs that we all have.

There's a more important reason, however, why Elijah needed two years of rest and relaxation. What lay ahead of him was going to be a stressful experience that most men never face in a dozen lifetimes. His encounter with the prophets of Baal at Mount Carmel would be one of the greatest challenges any prophet of God had faced since Moses did spiritual battle with the Pharaoh of Egypt. Elijah *needed* two years to get ready.

"A Cheerful Heart Is Good Medicine"

What did Elijah do for two years? After his isolation in the ravine, he probably spent a lot of time enjoying the young lad who had died and had come back to life. This probably did more for Elijah's emotional healing than anything God could have given him. To see the joy on his mother's face and seeing her faith in God grow each day brought healing to his soul. And since "a cheerful heart is good medicine" (Prov. 17:22), Elijah also experienced God's healing touch physically.

When the Time Arrived

When God once again spoke to Elijah directly, he was ready. Elijah was not surprised. We read: "After a long time, in the third year, the word of the LORD came to Elijah: 'Go and present yourself to Ahab, and I will send rain on the land.' So Elijah went to present himself to Ahab" (1 Kings 18:1–2).[1]

There's no hint of hesitancy in Elijah's response—no debate, no "ifs," "ands," or "buts." He knew this moment was coming—and that it had arrived! He was physically, emotionally, and spiritually ready.

An Old Friend

While Elijah was on his way to come face to face with Ahab, he met an old friend—a man named Obadiah. Though we don't know much about this man, what we learn in this encounter introduces us to a "giant in the faith" who can teach all of us some very dynamic lessons—particularly regarding how to survive in a pagan environment when you're committed to being a strong Christian. He is certainly among the unnamed "prophets" referred to in the Old Testament Hall of Faith outlined so dramatically in the New Testament (see Heb. 11:32).

In the Right Place at the Right Time

The Bible tells us two very important facts about Obadiah: (1) he "was in charge" of Ahab's palace, and (2) he "was a devout believer in the LORD" (1 Kings 18:3).

As you read through the Old Testament, you'll discover that God has always had key people in strategic positions just at the right time in order to accomplish His will for His people. Joseph became prime minister of Egypt when he was thirty years old. Because of this strategic position, he not only saved the Egyptians from a destructive famine; he was able to provide an environment where God could raise up the nation He had promised to Abraham.

Years later, Moses was in a strategic position in the same country, He was actually heir to the throne of Egypt—but this was not God's plan. He had to live forty years in the wilderness getting ready to come back to Egypt to deliver his people from captivity.

Daniel also emerged as one of the most influential men in the Babylonian and Medo-Persian empires. Nehemiah served as cupbearer to King Artaxerxes and, as result, led the children of Israel to rebuild the walls of Jerusalem. And we must not forget Esther, who, because of her strategic position in a pagan environment, saved her people from great persecution and potential annihilation.

Get the Picture?

In each case, God enabled key people to occupy important positions in the secular, pagan world in order to accomplish His divine purposes. In each instance, God used these individuals to accomplish His divine purposes through His chosen people—Israel.

An Incredible Combination

Add Obadiah to the list of individuals who occupied key positions by divine appointment. He was in charge of Ahab's palace. Think of it! He was the king's trusted administrator and confidant. He had open-ended responsibility and authority.

At the same time, Obadiah was a "believer in the LORD." But he was more! He "was a *devout* believer." He would not compromise his faith in the living God. In striking contrast to the king he served, Obadiah did not worship Baal—or any other false gods!

How was it possible for Obadiah to be in this strategic position, faithfully serving a king who was promoting the worst kind of pagan idolatry? More importantly, how could he be a devout believer? How was it possible to maintain Ahab's trust? How could he keep from being suspect?

Beyond Comprehension

The answers to these questions become even more mind-boggling when we discover Obadiah's undercover operations.

"While Jezebel was killing off the LORD's prophets," Obadiah was busy protecting them. He "had taken a hundred" of these men and had "hidden them in two caves, fifty in each." And note this! In the midst of the famine, he had "supplied them with food and water" (1 Kings 18:4).

Obadiah "fleshed out" his spiritual convictions in ways that are difficult to comprehend. His life had to hang in the balance every second of every twenty-four-hour day. Had someone in Ahab's palace become suspicious, it would have meant certain death for this man.

And what if one of Obadiah's servants had gotten disgruntled and "let the word slip out"? This was no cat-and-mouse game. This was a battle against Satan and his evil forces. Certainly, no one knew the danger more intensely than Obadiah. He made his choice deliberately and with the full knowledge that if he were caught, he would be executed on the spot.

What Motivated Obadiah?

What would cause a man to put both his strategic position and his life in jeopardy? The Scriptures give us the answer.

A Man of God

Obadiah "was a devout believer in the LORD." God was central in all he did. Obeying the Lord was far more important to Obadiah than anything else in life—including life itself. In this sense, he was a man just like Elijah!

A Man of Wisdom

Obadiah was not only a committed and courageous believer, but he was a very wise man. He had to be! Otherwise, he couldn't have filled such a strategic position in the king's palace and not gotten caught. In fact, it certainly took wisdom *beyond human ingenuity* to both develop and implement a plan to save the Lord's prophets. How Obadiah pulled this off, no one really knows. I am looking forward to meeting him in heaven someday and asking him to share with me all the exciting details. I'm confident Obadiah will begin the explanation by saying, "Without God, I could have done nothing."

"Is It Really You?"

The impact of the drought pressed in harder and harder on everyone—including Ahab. The king ordered Obadiah to help him find food for his horses and mules so he wouldn't have to kill them. Ironically, Ahab was more concerned about animals than people. So, the king went in one direction and Obadiah in the other, searching for springs and valleys where they might find some grass (see 1 Kings 18:4–6).

"As Obadiah was walking along, Elijah met him"—coming from the opposite direction. Obadiah immediately recognized Elijah, even though he hadn't seen him for three years. But needing reassurance, he asked, "Is it really you, my lord Elijah?" (v. 7).

Elijah's affirmation was certainly reassuring. It's hard to imagine what it was like to meet a fellow pilgrim who was committed to the same God. But Obadiah was not ready for Elijah's directive—"Go tell your master, 'Elijah is here'" (v. 8).

"Anything But That!"

The tension Obadiah had lived with for nearly three years exploded. He was defensive and fearful. "What have I done wrong," he asked, "that you are handing your servant over to Ahab to be put to death?" (v. 9).

Ever since the drought began to affect the economy in Israel, Ahab—influenced by Jezebel—had sent "secret service men" to every conceivable place in the kingdom to look for Elijah. And every person contacted had to sign a sworn confession that they had not seen Elijah nor did they know where he was.

We can now understand why Obadiah responded the way he did. For him to report back to Ahab that he had met Elijah but "had not brought him in" could lead to certain death. But even if Ahab responded positively and returned with Obadiah, he was still horribly frightened. "I don't know where the Spirit of the LORD may carry you when I leave you," he pleaded. "If I go and tell Ahab and he doesn't find you, he *will* kill me" (v. 12).

It Had Been a Tough Three Years

Obadiah's intense fear and frustration are understandable. He reminded Elijah of his faithfulness to God—serving and worshiping the Lord since his youth. With his heart pounding, he reviewed how he had jeopardized his own life *daily* by hiding the Lord's prophets in caves and providing them with food and water. "And now," he pleaded, "*now* you tell me to go to my master and say 'Elijah is here.' He will kill me!" (v, 14).

"Hey! Relax! I'll Be Here!"

Of all people, Elijah could understand and sympathize with Obadiah's predicament. In many respects, his task had been far more precarious than Elijah's. "As the LORD Almighty lives, whom I serve," Elijah said, "I will surely present myself to Ahab today" (v. 15).

We're not told what transpired between this courageous prophet and his faithful friend Obadiah after Elijah had reassured him that he would not disappear off the scene. We can only speculate. Elijah probably briefed him on all that had happened while he was in hiding—how God had cared for him and protected him. He certainly would have shared with Obadiah that God had made it clear that was the time to encounter Ahab face to face (see v. 1).

We're not told the extent to which Obadiah's fears dissipated. It could have happened quickly since he was used to this kind of tension. After all, he had lived consistently with fear in Ahab's court. But we do know that he was reassured. He responded to Elijah's directive. He returned to Ahab's palace and informed the king that Elijah was waiting to meet him. Ahab responded immediately and went to find Elijah. But that's another story!

Becoming God's Man Today

Principles to Live By

In the midst of this exciting story about Elijah, Obadiah suddenly stands out as a powerful example to Christian men who live and work in a secular—and often pagan—environment. He teaches all of us what we must do to be men of integrity.

Principle 1. God wants to use Christians who are in key positions in a secular and pagan society to accomplish His purpose in the world.

All of us need to remind ourselves why God left us in this world. Certainly, He wants to protect us. However, He has a purpose that is far more important than our safety and sense of security. God wants us to communicate His message of redemption. We are to be "salt and light"—as Jesus said (Matt. 5:13–14).

Building God's Kingdom

When we serve as dynamic witnesses in this world, we are building the kingdom of God—not a kingdom on this earth. The primary purpose is not to preserve our society. We are to glorify Him! Hopefully, we'll see renewal in our culture, but I'm convinced that this will only happen when we get our priorities straight and become men of integrity.

Praying for Those in Authority

God made this message clear in Paul's letter to Timothy. We are to make it a priority to pray "for kings and all those in authority, that we may live peaceful and quiet lives in all godliness and holiness" (1 Tim. 2:2). You see, God *is* interested in our protection and security—even in this world. However, that concern is secondary in the mind of God. Notice the reason we are to pray for government leaders! It is so that they might provide an environment where it is possible to share the good news of Jesus Christ. This is why Paul concludes his exhortation to pray for government leaders by saying, "This is good, and pleases God our Savior, *who wants all men to be saved* and to come to a knowledge of the truth" (2:3–4). Paul then succinctly states what it means to have this kind of knowledge: "For there is one God and one mediator between God and men, the man Christ Jesus, who gave himself as a ransom for all men" (1 Tim. 2:5–6).

Flesh and Blood Relationships

Every Christian who rubs shoulders with a non-Christian is in a strategic position. We can make our greatest influence, not through statements about morality, but through flesh-and-blood contacts with people. It's in these relationships that we can reflect our faith in God, our eternal hope for the future, and our love for God and one another. We can demonstrate our own morality and integrity. I believe God has set the stage for this message in our own culture. The world is deteriorating, leaving people to reap the results of their own moral choices. Consequently, many are searching frantically for something to give meaning to life.

As Christians, we have the answer to this dilemma. It's a personal relationship with Jesus Christ that gives hope for the present and the future. Furthermore, the answer involves loving, moral, and ethical relationships with other Christians. Not only can we flesh out our hope and security in Christ while we occupy our vocational positions on planet earth, but we can also encourage one another to continue to live in the good, acceptable, and perfect will of God (see Rom. 12:2).

Principle 2. God can only use Christians effectively in this world who are truly devoted to Him.

Obadiah illustrates this truth in an incredible way. He had served the Lord from his youth. And even if Ahab—the king he served—was a licentious idolater, Obadiah never compromised his integrity.

It's interesting that every biblical character who has occupied a strategic position in a secular environment and has been used by God in unusual ways has been this kind of person. Joseph would not compromise his moral convictions. Daniel disassociated himself from idolatry and continued to publicly worship God.

Win Their Respect

We'll never impress the world by being like them. Our value system must reflect God's standards of righteousness and holiness. Listen to the words of Peter: "Dear friends, I urge you, as aliens and strangers in the world, to abstain from sinful desires, which war against your soul. Live such good lives among the pagans that, though they accuse you of doing wrong, they may see your good deeds and glorify God on the day he visits us" (1 Pet. 2:11–12).

The apostle Peter is reminding us that it *is possible* to live for Christ and reflect His holiness—even in a pagan environment—without alienating unbelievers. They may not agree with us, but down deep they will respect us. They may laugh at us publicly but admire us privately. Though they may never say it to you, most non-Christians admire people who are willing to take a moral and ethical stand.

"Wise as Serpents and Harmless as Doves"

It's not always possible to avoid rejection and persecution. In fact, the Bible clearly states that if we are living as God wants us to live, we *will* be persecuted. However, there are Christians who alienate non-Christians unnecessarily. When this happens, it's not their spiritual convictions that brings a negative reaction, but how that spiritual conviction is communicated.

When Jesus sent His disciples out into a very hostile world, He said, "I am sending you out like sheep among wolves. Therefore be as shrewd as snakes and as innocent as doves" (Matt. 10:16).

We need to remind ourselves that even in Jerusalem—where Jesus was hated and crucified—when Jews became Christians and lived as God wanted them to live, they were "enjoying the favor of all the people." Thousands came to Christ because unbelievers admired their dynamic and loving relationships (see Acts 2:41–47).

Principle 3. God uses Christians in a special way who reflect wisdom in their relationships with non-Christians.

There are lots of illustrations today of Christians who are not acting wisely in their efforts to counteract the current evil trends in our society. Their approach is bombastic and offensive. Their behavior is defiant and overly aggressive.

Don't misunderstand! I'm not suggesting that we compromise our convictions. Rather, we should follow Paul's instructions to Timothy:

> Don't have anything to do with foolish and stupid arguments, because you know they produce quarrels. And the LORD's servant must not quarrel; instead, he must *be kind to everyone*, able to teach, not resentful. Those who oppose him he must gently instruct, in the hope that God will grant them repentance leading them to a knowledge of the truth, and that they will come to their senses and escape from the trap of the devil, who has taken them captive to do his will. (2 Tim. 2:23–26)

Don't Respond Out of Fear

Many Christians respond negatively because they are threatened. When fear takes over, we become more emotional than rational. Unfortunately, we end up violating biblical principles of communication—which always causes non-Christians to respond in anger. When that happens, we've lost our platform for effective communication. The message of Christ and salvation is lost in the battle.

Misdirected Commitment

Christians are often "devout"—but devout in the wrong way. Their "devotion" is reflected in aggressive attitudes and actions toward non-Christians. For example, I've known of Christian leaders who have gone to prison because they've refused to meet government health standards for conducting Christian schools. They openly defied the laws of our society that are designed to protect our children from unnecessary harm.

Please understand. They were not reacting against laws that violated their moral and spiritual convictions. They were not being asked to do things that were contrary to *God's laws!* Rather, they were reacting to government requirements designed to protect our children from danger. In this instance, their actions were a direct violation of Peter's exhortation— "Submit yourselves for the LORD's sake to every authority instituted among men" (1 Pet. 2:13).

What About Abortion?

Personally, I believe abortion is murder. It was a sad, sad day when our government legalized this terrible practice. I want to do everything I can to convince people this is a sin and that God will judge us for it. As a pastor, I preach against it from the pulpit. At the same time, I preach God's love and forgiveness for those who have sinned.

I want to do all I can to reverse these horrible laws in our society. I also want to help women make proper choices— never to abort their children (unless, of course, their own life is in danger).

However, I cannot condone attacking this evil in our society with "lawbreaking" tactics. Though I, in many respects, admire those who are willing to be incarcerated for their convictions, I question their methodology. Thank God, there are yet many opportunities to combat this evil through legitimate channels. It's my personal opinion that we need to be very diligent in exhausting these possibilities.

There Will Come a Time

I'm convinced there will come a time in our "free society" when as Christians we must refuse to cooperate with the government. When asked to do something that violates the Word of God, we must not compromise. Like many Christians in the early centuries, we may need to choose death rather than violate our spiritual convictions.

Fortunately, none of us have ever been asked to deny that Jesus Christ is our Lord and Master, but many in the New Testament world were. However, even in this kind of situation, these believers responded in a Christlike way. They were not defiant. Many went to their death submissively and without anger toward those who caused it. Like Jesus Christ, they said, "Father, forgive them, for they do not know what they are doing" (Luke 23:34). Stephen certainly illustrates this as an imitator of His Lord (see Acts 7:59–60).

What About Our Tax Dollars?

Some Christians have advocated that it would be perfectly right to refuse to pay taxes because our government leaders are spending our money in immoral and unethical ways. There is one major problem with this kind of thinking. Jesus Christ told His disciples to "give to Caesar what is Caesar's, and to God what is God's" (Matt. 22:21). Jesus issued this command with full realization that the Roman emperors and leaders were guilty of horrible crimes against humanity. Furthermore, their personal lifestyles reeked with immorality. Don't forget that Herod actually had John the Baptist beheaded because his wife hated this bold and powerful prophet who preached against Herod's own sin.

What Must We Do?

It's certainly understandable why many Christians in our culture are nervous. Our social values have changed—and are changing even more. It's impacting our children. In fact, it's leading our whole society down the road to destruction.

However, we must remember that God is still God. He is the sovereign Lord of the universe. He is still in control. We can trust Him. Furthermore, one of the lessons we can learn from Obadiah is that we must not react in unwise ways to bring changes in our culture. If we do, we'll be violating the commands and the principles of Scripture. Furthermore, it often makes our witness in this world ineffective.

Principle 4. God delights in using our predicaments to achieve His purposes.

Where there are no difficult problems, there is no need for divine solutions. Where there are no battles against evil, there are no spiritual victories. Conversely, when we face predicaments that seem to be beyond our abilities to handle, it's during these times that God often reveals His power and His love. It's in the midst of persecution that God enables us to truly reveal our commitment and love for Jesus Christ. When we're tempted the most, we can bear witness to God's power to deliver us.

Listen to the words of Paul: "Everyone who wants to live a godly life in Christ Jesus will be persecuted." When we're truly living for Christ, there will be some at least who will do everything they can to hurt us.

This should not surprise us. In fact, Paul went on to say that "evil men and impostors will go from bad to worse, deceiving and being deceived" (2 Tim. 3:12–13).

God Can Turn Lemons into Lemonade

It shouldn't alarm us then when we find ourselves in predicaments because of our integrity. These are God's opportunities to demonstrate through us His presence in our lives. He has a unique way of turning "lemons into lemonade" and "stumbling blocks into stepping-stones."

There will be times, of course, when we become fearful and frustrated—just like Obadiah. There will be times when we need reassurance and encouragement—just like Obadiah.

There will be times when we feel there is no solution to the problem—just like Obadiah. But there *was* a solution! God's purpose was fulfilled. Certainly, God can do the same for us—and through us.

Becoming a Man of Integrity

As you use the following questions to evaluate your life, circle the proper number. Ask the Holy Spirit to impress on your heart one thing you need to do to develop more integrity in your life. Then write out a specific goal. For example, you may be reacting in an inappropriate way to those around you who are demonstrating anything but integrity. You need to develop a proactive approach to these problems and see them as opportunities to demonstrate Jesus Christ in your life.

1. To what extent am I allowing God to use me to accomplish His purposes in this world . . .

	Not at all				Sometimes				Always	
➤ on the job?	1	2	3	4	5	6	7	8	9	10
➤ in my neighborhood?	1	2	3	4	5	6	7	8	9	10
➤ at school?	1	2	3	4	5	6	7	8	9	10
➤ in my recreational and social activities?	1	2	3	4	5	6	7	8	9	10
➤ other?	1	2	3	4	5	6	7	8	9	10

2. To what extent am I living a devoted life for Jesus Christ, and at the same time being wise and tactful in my relationships with non-Christians?

Not at all   Sometimes   Always

1   2   3   4   5   6   7   8   9   10

3. To what extent do I view predicaments as God's opportunities to demonstrate His power and love through my life?

Not at all   Sometimes   Always

1 2 3 4 5 6 7 8 9 10

Set a Goal

With God's help, I will begin immediately to carry out the following goal in my life:

_____

_____

_____

_____

Memorize the Following Scripture

Dear friends, I urge you, as aliens and strangers in the world, to abstain from sinful desires, which war against your soul. Live such good lives among the pagans that, though they accuse you of doing wrong, they may see your good deeds and glorify God on the day he visits us.

1 PETER 2:11–12

Chapter 6

Avoiding Rationalization
Read 1 Kings 18:16–19 and 21

Someone has said that "rationalization" is a mental technique which allows you to be unfair to others without feeling guilty.

I like this definition. However, it is simplistic. There's more. Rationalization is a means of self-deception. Sigmund Freud first popularized this psychological concept—along with a number of other defense mechanisms we supposedly use to handle anxiety.

What Can We Learn from an Atheist?

Freud was anything but Christian in his thinking and lifestyle; in fact, he claimed to be an atheist. Yet he saw something in human beings that God said existed long before modern psychology appeared on the scene. Man's heart *is* deceitful! Freud saw this in his own life. It's been that way ever since Adam and Eve used rationalization to handle their guilt and anxiety following their sin in the garden of Eden.

Some rationalizations, of course, are rather benign. Moreover, they may help us survive emotionally in some situations. But self-deception is never totally harmless. It may indicate a more serious problem.

For example, I've always been involved in athletic activities. I love to compete—and to win! You name it—basketball, volleyball, or racquetball (one of my favorite sports since I've gotten older). But, when I lose, I never cease to be amazed at how quickly I can find an excuse for losing. Why? It's the natural way to handle the anxiety we're feeling because of a wounded ego. Can anyone identify?

This may not be a major problem, but it can reflect how insecure we really feel. It may also indicate deeper problems in our personalities. The more we walk out of the will of God, the more serious our rationalizations become.

King Ahab Is Exhibit "A"

Imagine the look on Ahab's face when Obadiah reported that he had met Elijah. The king had been combing the country for more than three years looking for this man who had plagued Israel with a drought. Imagine, too, his surprise when Obadiah informed him that Elijah was waiting to meet him. Whatever Ahab's emotional reactions, he was on his way immediately!

"Is That You, You Troubler of Israel?"

What a rationalization! When Ahab asked this question, he was reflecting a deep-rooted problem that has affected all of us—a social disease that has infected every man and woman who has ever lived on planet earth. Ever since sin entered the human race, we've tended to shift the blame for our own irresponsible actions to someone else. This is a classic illustration of rationalization.

Where Did It All Start?

"Lord, It Was the Woman You Gave Me!"

Earlier I made reference to what happened in the garden of Eden. Let's take a closer look! Adam was the first man to ever rationalize his wrongdoing. God had confronted him in the garden after he and Eve had disobeyed. Note Adam's response after he and Eve had eaten from the tree they were told to avoid: "The *woman* you put here with me—she gave me some fruit from the tree, and I ate it" (Gen. 3:12). Actually, Adam was not only shifting the blame to Eve, but he indulged in what we might call the *ultimate* rationalization—putting the blame for our actions on God. Though he referred to Eve in his response, he made it clear that it was God who gave her to him. Who then was to blame?

"The Devil Made Me Do It!"

Eve also rationalized. When the Lord asked her what *she* had done, she replied, "The serpent deceived me, and I ate" (3:13). In other words, "the devil made me do it!" She shifted the blame to Satan.

That Culprit Called "Fear"

What was the primary driving force behind this rationalization in the garden of Eden? When Adam was confronted by God, he gave the real reason: "I was afraid" (v. 10). Ever since that moment, fear has often been at the root of our rationalizations.

It shouldn't surprise us, then, that all of us have difficulty facing the negative consequences of our irresponsible personal attitudes and actions. It's a direct result of the spiritual disease the Bible identifies as sin. And, as happened so many years ago, one of the primary manifestations of sin in our lives is fear—fear of rejection, fear of punishment, fear of facing the consequences of our own actions. There's no doubt about it. Fear causes us to rationalize.

"You Are Responsible for the Wrong I Am Suffering"

Ever since Adam and Eve introduced us to this natural tendency, the problem of rationalization crops up in human relationships.

Remember Abraham and Sarah? When she was unable to bear children, she sold her husband on the idea to have a child by her maidservant, Hagar. Strange and immoral? To us, yes! But this was a common practice in the pagan world of Abraham's day. In fact, marriage contracts often included a clause stipulating that if a wife could not bear children, she would be responsible to provide a substitute woman who could. Carrying on the family name was a priority.

Sarah's Rationalization

Abraham willingly cooperated with Sarah's plan. There seemed to be no resistance at all. Sure enough, Hagar bore him a son. But things didn't turn out as Sarah had hoped—and as Abraham had planned. When the maidservant became pregnant, "she began to despise her mistress" (Gen. 16:4). Like her first "parents"—and ours—Sarah would not acknowledge her mistake and take the blame. "You are responsible for the wrong I am suffering," she said to her husband. "I put my servant in your arms, and now that she knows she is pregnant, she despises me" (v. 5).

Jealousy—Another Emotional Culprit

Sarah illustrated another primary reason we rationalize—*jealousy*—and its accompanying emotion, *anger*. How quickly this combination of feelings can take over in our lives and cause us to blame others for our own actions!

I am reminded of a woman who nagged her husband to buy her a new home. Another woman in the church—someone she didn't particularly like—had just moved into a new place and she didn't want to be outdone. Frankly, she was jealous.

Against his better judgment, the husband gave in and secured a loan that put them both in a very risky position—even with his present level of income. Then he lost his job and had to settle for a lower salary in another company.

Unfortunately, they lost their home. But even more tragic, the wife blamed her husband for their predicament. If he hadn't lost his job—which was beyond his control since a number of people were laid off because of restructuring—they wouldn't be in this predicament. This, of course, is a classic case of rationalization—putting the blame on someone else.

"Out Came This Calf!"

When Moses ascended Mount Sinai to receive the Ten Commandments, the children of Israel grew restless and inpatient. Revealing the depth of their carnality, they asked Aaron to make them some gods that would lead them into the promised land. "As for this fellow Moses who brought us up out of Egypt," they complained, "we don't know what has happened to him" (Exod. 32:1).

It's always been a surprise to me that Aaron responded. He molded a golden calf and built an altar. He then allowed the people to bow down to this false god and to offer sacrifices. They even committed sexual immorality as a part of their worship. Clearly they had carried over into their experience in the wilderness what they had observed and participated in while in Egypt.

"You Know How Prone These People Are to Evil"

God was extremely angry with His people. Here He was giving their leader, Moses, the Ten Commandments. God had brought them safely out of Egypt and across the Red Sea. He had already cared for their physical needs in the wilderness. He was ready to judge His people severely.

Moses reasoned with the Lord and asked Him not to judge Israel so severely. God relented! However, Moses then was faced with the responsibility to confront his brother, Aaron, with what he had done.

Aaron's rationalization is absolutely incredible—"Do not be angry, my lord," Aaron pleaded with Moses. "You know how prone these people are to evil. They said to me, 'Make us gods who will go before us. As for this fellow Moses who brought us up out of Egypt, we don't know what has happened to him.' So I told them, 'Whoever has any gold jewelry, take it off.' Then they gave me the gold, and I threw it into the fire, and *out came this calf!*" (32:22–24).

Rather than admitting that he had sinned, Aaron shifted the blame to his fellow Israelites. True, they had asked him to do it. But the facts are, he cooperated. Furthermore, he came up with the incredible explanation that the calf somehow emerged from the fire without his help. This was a bold-faced lie since the Scriptures record that "he took what they handed him and made it into an idol cast in the shape of a calf, *fashioning it with a tool*" (v. 4). No wonder Jeremiah wrote, "The heart is deceitful above all things and beyond cure. Who can understand it?" (Jer. 17:9).

Prestige and Power

Like Adam and Eve, Aaron certainly experienced *fear*. But, in his case, there's more to the story. Initially, he certainly had to be motivated by his need for *prestige* and *power*. He had an opportunity to lead Israel. The people catered to his ego by asking him to step in and take Moses' place. After all, he probably didn't feel good operating in his brother's shadow.

When Moses confronted Aaron with his sin, we see an interesting blend of feelings. He was certainly afraid since he obviously knew how displeased the Lord was with his actions. All of these emotions blended to motivate him to respond in the way he did.

"My Soldiers Did It"

When Saul was anointed king, the Lord instructed him to destroy the Amalekites because they had mercilessly attacked the children of Israel in the wilderness. He was to spare nothing —including their "cattle and sheep, camels and donkeys" (1 Sam. 15:3).

Sadly, Saul disobeyed the Lord. He kept "the best of . . . everything that was good" (v. 9). The Lord was unhappy—

and so was Samuel. In his grief, Samuel went to see Saul and confronted him with his disobedience.

Even if you've never read this story, by now I'm sure you can guess what Saul did. He rationalized by shifting the blame to his men. He told Samuel that *"the soldiers* brought them from the Amalekites; *they* spared the best of the sheep and cattle to sacrifice to the LORD your God" (v. 15).

Again, this was a lie. The scriptural text makes it very clear that it was both "Saul" and his "army" that spared "everything that was good" (v. 9).

Another Culprit—Our Pride

Following his disobedience, Saul immediately went to Carmel and "set up a monument *in his own honor"* (v. 12). He was motivated by *pride*.

Pride and ego are certainly at the root of most rationalizations. It certainly helps explain why Adam blamed Eve, why Eve blamed Satan, why Sarah blamed Abraham, and why Aaron blamed the people. And very clearly, it explains why Saul blamed his army.

"You Are the Man!"

King David illustrates unbelievable rationalization and how to deal with it both negatively and positively. He certainly rationalized away his sin when he committed adultery and murder. But when he was confronted with his sin, his heart was still sensitive toward God and he responded by admitting that what he had done was terribly wrong. In short, he stopped rationalizing (see Ps. 51).

"One Little Ewe Lamb"

The Lord had sent Nathan to confront David. Ironically, his approach was far more subtle than Elijah's approach to Ahab. He told David a story about a rich man who "had a very large number of sheep and cattle." By contrast, there was a poor

man who "had nothing except a little ewe lamb he had bought."
Nathan went on to explain to David that the little lamb was very
special to this man. "He raised it, and it grew up with him and
his children. It shared his food, drank from his cup and even
slept in his arms. It was like a daughter to him" (2 Sam 12:2–3).

By this time, Nathan had tapped David's deepest emotions. He no doubt remembered the days when he was alone
as a young shepherd boy caring for little lambs. But it was at
this point that Nathan began to drive home the message that
he was trying to get across to David. He went on to explain
that one day a man was traveling through and stopped at the
rich man's home for a meal. Rather than "taking one of his
own sheep or cattle to prepare a meal for the traveler . . . he
took the ewe lamb that belonged to the poor man and prepared it for the one who had come to him" (v. 4).

"The Man Deserves to Die!"

Ironically, David was angry. Again, his shepherd heart
took over. He could identify emotionally. How often he must
have held a little ewe lamb in his arms, perhaps even feeding it
from his own cup and sleeping at night holding it in his arms.
"As surely as the LORD lives," David responded, "the man who
did this deserves to die!" (v. 5).

David was totally caught off guard by Nathan's response.
"You are the man!" (v. 7) he said. As the king of Israel, David
had been guilty of an even greater crime. He had taken away
Bathsheba, Uriah's *only* wife, while he had *many*. At that
point, Nathan pronounced judgment on David for his sin.

"I Have Sinned"

Nathan's words penetrated David's heart like a knife. "I
have sinned against the LORD," he cried (v. 13). His rationalization, motivated by lust and fear, turned to brutal honesty.
He faced the reality of what he had done. He made no excuses,
but threw himself upon God's mercy. What a different response
from that of Ahab!

"I Am Innocent of This Man's Blood!"

When Pilate "took water and washed his hands in front of the crowd" that was crying out for Jesus' blood, we have the most dramatic illustration of rationalization in all of Scripture. He was responsible under Roman law to make a decision regarding Jesus Christ. However, he by his own admission, could find "no fault" in Jesus. But, because he feared the people, he "handed him over to be crucified" (Matt. 27:26). Thinking he could clear himself, he cried out, "I am innocent of this man's blood. It is *your* responsibility!" (v. 24).

Pilate had just turned a perfect Man—the God-man, Jesus Christ—over to an unruly crowd to be put to death. However, in his own mind, he had convinced himself he wasn't to blame. He was attempting to relieve his own conscience of the guilt that was gripping his soul.

Guilt is another emotion that leads many people to rationalize, particularly Christians. Since our conscience has been enlightened by the Holy Spirit, our guilt level goes higher because we *know* that we are violating the will of God.

Personally, I believe King Ahab knew the truth. Furthermore, I don't believe he had a seared conscience. True, he had failed God miserably. Probably not a day went by that he did not struggle with his guilt. He had a choice: admit it or blame someone else for the problems in the kingdom. He chose to allow guilt (and other emotions) to cause him to shift the blame to Elijah. That's why he asked, "Is that you, you troubler of Israel?" (1 Kings 18:17).

Scratch an Adult and You'll Find a Child

King Ahab rationalized because of a number of factors. That's usually true with all of us. However, there seem to be some unique factors in this king's personality that gives us additional insights as to why he could rationalize so easily.

Take the experience Ahab had with a man by the name of Naboth. This man owned a vineyard that was located near

Ahab's palace. Ahab admired the location and he wanted it for a vegetable garden. Being halfway decent, he offered to buy the vineyard—or to replace it with another one in a different location.

"Why Are You So Sullen?"

The particular vineyard was special to Naboth. He had received it as an inheritance. Consequently, he—perhaps naively—rejected the king's offer, which made Ahab "sullen and angry" (21:4). Would you believe that Ahab went home, threw himself across his bed and sulked! He even "refused to eat" (v. 4). Jezebel was puzzled by his behavior and asked him, "Why are you so sullen? Why won't you eat?" (v. 5).

When Ahab explained what had happened, Jezebel took over. With her evil mind, she devised a scheme to have Naboth accused of blasphemy against both God and the king. As a result, he was killed. Ahab then took possession of the vineyard (see v. 16).

That Culprit Called "Self-Centeredness"

What a sad commentary on Ahab's personality! He was incredibly selfish and horribly spoiled. In this particular story, we see a weak, passive man who acted more like a child than an adult.

Think of it! Here was the king of Israel—who was wealthier than any other man in the nation—sulking because he couldn't have a poor man's vineyard to turn into a vegetable garden.

Elijah's No-Nonsense Response

Against this backdrop, we can now understand more fully Ahab's charge against Elijah—accusing the prophet of the problems in Israel. Elijah dealt with this rationalization head-on. "'I have not made trouble for Israel,' Elijah replied. 'But you and your father's family have. You have abandoned the LORD's commands and have followed the Baals'" (18:18).

Elijah then challenged Ahab to a contest on Mount

Carmel. "Now summon the people from all over Israel to meet me on Mount Carmel," he said. "And bring the four hundred and fifty prophets of Baal and the four hundred prophets of Asherah, who eat at Jezebel's table" (v. 19).

Truth Must Prevail!

Elijah's response illustrates how serious rationalization must be dealt with—in others and in ourselves. It must be confronted—sometimes directly, sometimes indirectly. But, if we're going to stop rationalizing, truth must prevail. Self-deception must be exposed.

Unfortunately, Ahab would not listen to Elijah. He was too proud, too arrogant—and had convinced himself that he could do battle with the God of Abraham, Isaac, and Jacob, and win! What self-deception! He was headed for a humiliating defeat and eventually death. Sadly, he would take a number of people down with him.

Becoming God's Man Today

Principles to Live By

All of us are capable of rationalizing to one degree or another. As we've seen from several scriptural illustrations, there are a number of reasons why we blame others for our irresponsible behavior.

Principle 1. Is It Fear?

Ever since Adam and Eve rationalized because of fear, so do we. Husbands blame wives and wives blame husbands. Parents blame children and children blame parents. We blame one another and God for our irresponsible behavior.

God, however, does not want us to be afraid of Him. His wrath fell on His Son, Jesus Christ, who bore the sins of the whole world. Consequently, His perfect love is available to everyone of us. Rather than blaming others for our human weaknesses, we should face reality, confess our sins, and accept forgiveness in Jesus Christ.

How Fear Affects Children

Young children often rationalize out of fear because of adults who are insensitive and too severe in their discipline. When this happens, I believe God holds us as parents responsible. We should be mature enough to understand the natural bent in a child's personality (see Prov. 22:6). We do not want to be responsible for our children growing up to be rationalizers because we have created a fearful environment.

Don't Blame Your Parents

There comes a time, however, when every human being is responsible for his own behavior—no matter what the cause. We must not go through life blaming our parents for making us the way we are. They may have made mistakes, but we are responsible not to continue to rationalize away our irresponsible actions because of their mistakes.

Principle 2. Is It Jealousy?

Jealousy is a withering emotion. It strangles our souls and alienates us from others. Jealousy appears early in life. In fact, as children develop the capacity to show affection, they also develop the capacity to be jealous. These feelings are often twin emotions—one positive and the other negative. Since this emotion appears so early in children, as parents we must be cautious not to show favoritism to one child or the other. This is what happened with Isaac and Rebekah. Isaac favored Esau and Rebekah favored Jacob. The results were disastrous.

Jealousy is also a very strong emotion. Like fear, it's often at the root of rationalization. For example, Joe is always criticizing Bob for the way he does things—the way he talks, the way he dresses, the way he relates to others. In actuality, Joe resents Bob's ability to speak. He also resents the fact that Bob is asked to speak more often than he is. Joe is jealous—but won't admit it to himself or others. His rationalization is seen in that he always makes Bob the focus of the problem—not his own emotional struggle.

Principle 3. Is It Anger?

All of us do things we regret because of anger. But when it happens, it's difficult to admit why and oftentimes we blame our irresponsible actions on others—or on other reasons.

For example, Bill frequently loses his temper. When he does, he feels terrible. But rather than admitting the problem and asking for forgiveness, he blames his quick-temperedness on his ill health. It's amazing how often he "develops" a headache *after* he loses his temper rather than *before*. In other words, he often "becomes ill" *after* he goes out of control in order to justify his aggressive behavior.

Not All Anger Is Sin

Anger is a difficult emotion to handle since it's such a normal emotion. It's also difficult for many Christians because we've been taught that we should never get angry. However, that's not good biblical teaching. Paul stated, "In your anger, do not sin" (Eph. 4:26).

Here the apostle is acknowledging that we all get angry, but when we do, he is exhorting us not to allow that anger to become sinful. Consequently, he goes on to state, "Do not let the sun go down while you are still angry, and do not give the devil a foothold" (vv. 26b–27).

When Anger Becomes Sinful

Anger definitely becomes sinful when it lingers and turns into bitterness. But it also becomes sinful when we allow it to cause us to rationalize. To keep this from happening, James gives us some great wisdom when he wrote that all of us should be "quick to listen, slow to speak and slow to become angry, for man's anger does not bring about the righteous life that God desires" (James 1:19–20).

Principle 4. Is It a Need for Security?

Every time Jim is afraid of failure, he comes up with numerous reasons why he shouldn't participate in a particular activity. Either he is too busy, too tired, or "too something else." Unable to face his real problem, he gives what sounds like a legitimate and socially acceptable reason for avoiding the situation.

I grew up in Indiana and played a lot of basketball. Frankly, I was pretty good at it. However, later in life I shifted to volleyball. It was a brand new game for me. I had to learn a whole new set of skills. Consequently, I often made a lot of mistakes. I remember how much it bothered me when my teammates purposely constructed plays to avoid my participation in the game—even though I was on the court.

What a humiliating experience! I often remember saying in my mind—if not out loud—"If we were only playing basketball." In actuality, I was rationalizing because of my insecurity and a related emotion, pride—which leads us to our next question.

Principle 5. Is It Pride and Ego?

I suppose more people rationalize because of pride or a wounded ego than any other reason. This should not surprise us. It caused Satan's downfall.

Whenever we fail at something, we become ego involved. Like me, John is a classic example. He was a good athlete and intensely competitive—as most men are. But he often plays tennis with men who outclass him. When he loses, he always makes excuses. Often he is "out of shape," or "didn't get much sleep the night before," or "he had something on his mind."

Don't misunderstand! Some of these things may be true—but he will never admit that the other person is just a better tennis player than he is. John's problem is pride combined with a sense of insecurity.

Principle 6. Is It Guilt?

Guilt is a subtle emotion and hard to detect. It's often associated with some type of obsessive, compulsive behavior. Pilate "washed his hands" when he turned the innocent Son of God over to a howling mob to be crucified. Today some people do the same thing to cover up their guilt. Activities that involve some type of "cleansing" often become a means of demonstrating this kind of rationalization. Or, a person may become excessively neat, tidy, and organized. Don't misunderstand. Some people are just more concerned about cleanliness or they're just more organized. However, when this becomes obsessive in a person's life, there may be deeper roots to the problems.

I know of a man who spent day after day washing his car. Even though it was virtually spotless, he still continued to go through his "car-washing ritual!" This kind of behavior is often motivated by guilt that has been repressed from consciousness.

Some people engage in this kind of obsessive-compulsive behavior because of *false* guilt. This kind of behavior often begins in childhood because of parents who are too strict— who expect too much. Sometimes it relates to being a part of a legalistic religious system that has developed a standard of conduct that is cultural rather than biblical.

When this happens, a person needs help in "tuning" his conscience to God's standard of conduct rather than a "man-made" set of rules. To do this, we need to gain insights into our own personalities. We need help—preferably from a sensitive Christian counselor who understands these internal dynamics.

Principle 7. Is It Selfishness?

Some people blame others for crises and problems in their lives simply because they are self-centered and egocentric. There's no other explanation. They believe the whole world revolves around themselves. No matter what happens, if it makes them look bad, they put the blame on someone else. They never accept their share of responsibility.

Self-centered people take advantage of others and they're never satisfied with what they have. This was certainly true of Ahab.

Principle 8. Is It Lust?

Physical and psychological appetites can lead to incredible rationalization. For example, some Christians justify exposing themselves to carnal experiences in order to discover what is "going on in the world." After all, how can they be effective witnesses without knowing how the world lives?

To a certain extent this may be true. However, this reality makes it even easier to rationalize. A true test of our motives is the extent we want more and more exposure to the world's system. More than likely, when this happens, people are simply justifying their fleshly appetites by giving an acceptable reason that is really not acceptable to themselves. Someone has said, "We don't have to swim in a sewer to smell it"—to know it's there and why it stinks!

Becoming an Honest Man

All of us must be on guard against rationalizing. Being a Christian does not exempt us from this sin. What makes it so difficult is that it is painful to be honest with ourselves. Furthermore, we can be deceived without knowing it. That's why it is so important to listen carefully to the "voice of God" through the Word of God.

How do we overcome this problem? First we must acknowledge with Jeremiah that "the heart is deceitful above all things and beyond cure. Who can understand it?" The answer, of course, is that God can. He can cure us of our sin. Jeremiah acknowledged that when he wrote, "I the LORD search the heart and examine the mind" (Jer. 17:9–10). God knows our hearts—and He wants us to know our hearts as well.

Remember, too, that "the word of God is living and active." It is "sharper than any double-edged sword, it penetrates even to dividing soul and spirit, joints and marrow; it judges the thoughts and attitudes of the heart" (Heb. 4:12).

David gives us a model prayer for getting to know ourselves. He prayed: "Search me, O God, and know my heart;

test me and know my anxious thoughts. See if there is any offensive way in me, and lead me in the way everlasting" (Ps. 139:23–24). Be assured, God will answer this prayer when you pray it sincerely!

Finally, pray and ask the Holy Spirit to help you discern areas of rationalization and what emotions cause this rationalization. Once you've worked through the following exercise, write out a specific goal. For example, you may discover that you rationalize frequently because you are afraid of failure.

Ask Yourself These Questions

1. When was the last time you rationalized your attitudes and actions and blamed someone else for your irresponsible behavior? What were those attitudes and actions?

2. What caused you to rationalize?

- ➤ Fear
- ➤ Jealousy
- ➤ Anger
- ➤ Fear of failure
- ➤ Pride
- ➤ Guilt
- ➤ Selfishness
- ➤ Lust
- ➤ Other _____

Take Some Action Steps

- ➤ Confess your sin to God.
- ➤ Accept His forgiveness.
- ➤ Acknowledge your rationalization to the person or persons you've tried to deceive.
- ➤ Decide by God's grace to deal with the cause and to avoid self-deception and rationalization.

➤ Read the Word of God regularly and ask God to help you to live an honest, upright life.

Seek Professional Help If Needed

If you are sincerely trying to overcome your problem through confessions, prayer, and obedience to the Word of God—and yet cannot experience victory—your problem may be more psychological than spiritual. If you feel this is the case, seek help from a competent Christian counselor who can help you understand and overcome your problem.

Ironically, when we discover that our problems are sometimes caused by psychological reasons, it increases our tendency to rationalize rather than delivering us from this problem. What makes this so subtle is that it's easier to blame our problem on "psychological causes" rather than face the fact that we must bear final responsibility for our actions. For example, if our problems are more psychological than spiritual, the roots may go back to our relationship with our parents. It becomes easy to start blaming them for our present behavior and go right on behaving irresponsibly. If we do, we have replaced one rationalization with another.

Set a Goal

With God's help, I will begin immediately to carry out the following goal in my life:

_____

_____

_____

_____

Memorize the Following Scripture

Search me, O God, and know my heart;
test me and know my anxious thoughts.
See if there is any offensive way in me,
and lead me in the way everlasting.
PSALM 139:23–24

Chapter 7

Avoiding Double-Mindedness
Read Genesis 19:1–26 and 1 Kings 18:19–21

I grew up in a religious community that eventually led me to be a "double-minded" person. In actuality, I didn't face this tension until I began to discover the truth. My difficulty lay in making a choice between what was primarily cultural and what was biblical. This "emotional war" went on in my soul for several years—sometimes raging, sometimes reflecting "minor skirmishes"—but my mind was always in a state of "alertness" ready to do battle with the issues that divided my heart.

Though my double-mindedness was far different than Israel's when Elijah challenged them at Mount Carmel, there are some similarities, particularly in terms of being spiritually unstable and indecisive. This should not surprise us since James states that "a double-minded man" is "unstable in all he does" (James 1:8).

A Direct Message to Elijah

When God spoke to Elijah while he was residing in Zarephath, the message was detailed and very direct! He was to go immediately and present himself to Ahab (see 1 Kings 18:1). Though we are only given a brief sketch of what Elijah was to do, the details were clear to this prophet. Elijah knew what lay ahead. Though he was walking by faith, it was faith based on the Lord's direct revelation. At some point in time, God told him exactly what he was to do on Mount Carmel (see v. 36).

This does not mean that Elijah was always clear-minded. His wilderness experience was often difficult, filled with lonely days, sleepless nights, fearful moments, and periods of doubt and uncertainty. However, the fog that sometimes clouded his soul had now lifted. He was prepared to face not only Ahab and the prophets of Baal and Asherah, but his people Israel.

"Meet Me on Mount Carmel"

When Elijah met King Ahab, he immediately issued a challenge. This was not the time to discuss options. Elijah threw down the gauntlet and was perfectly confident who was about to win the battle. "Now summon the people from all over Israel to meet me on Mount Carmel. And bring the four hundred and fifty prophets of Baal and the four hundred prophets of Asherah, who eat at Jezebel's table" (v. 19).

A Message for All Israel

God designed the dramatic contest that lay ahead, not primarily for the false prophets, but for His deluded people. The prophets of Baal and Asherah would merely serve as a means in God's hands to demonstrate to Israel their false theology, their meaningless rituals, and their evil ways. The Lord wanted His people to see for themselves that they were being led astray.

Ahab's Naïveté

For some incredible reason, Ahab thought he could handle Elijah's challenge. He issued an order for the children of Israel to climb Mount Carmel. We don't know how many people responded but it must have been a great multitude. They all knew something unusual was going to happen. Some were probably angry, some fearful, some confused, but one thing is certain. They were *all* curious! The majority were probably highly motivated to come just to catch a glimpse of this prophet of God who was responsible for the drought that plagued Israel for three and a half years.

Most, no doubt, knew of Ahab's fruitless search for Elijah. Perhaps they thought that Ahab had finally succeeded. Whatever their knowledge and emotional state of mind, they did not realize that they were going to see a demonstration of God's power that would affect their lives for years to come.

The World's Largest Stage

The top of Mount Carmel was a perfect place for this contest. It was about to become a great outdoor theater that would accommodate thousands of people. The "stage" would become the largest in the world. Over one thousand actors could perform at the same time—though only the four hundred prophets of Baal responded to Ahab's order. The specific location was at a place called el-Mohraka. Robert Jamieson, in his commentary on 1 Kings, graphically describes the setting:

> Mount Carmel is a bold, bluff promontory. . . . It is a long range, presenting many summits and intersected by a number of small ravines. The spot where the contest took place is situated at the eastern extremity, which is also the highest point of the whole ridge. It is called el-Mohraka, "the Burning," or "the Burnt Place." No spot could have been better adapted for the thousands of Israel to have stood, drawn up on those gentle slopes. The rock shoots up in an almost perpendicular wall of more than 200 feet in height. . . . This wall made it visible over the whole plain, and from all its surrounding heights, where gazing multitudes would be stationed."[1]

How Long Will You Waver?

We're not told how long it took the people to finally gather in front of this "huge stage." It may have taken several days. But when they all arrived, Elijah issued his challenge. Going before the people, he must have mustered all of the energy at his disposal and cried out, "How long will you waver between two opinions? If the LORD is God, follow him; but if Baal is God, follow him" (1 Kings 18:21).

There were still two opinions among the children of Israel. If there had not been, Elijah wouldn't have asked the question. The majority probably still believed in the God of their fathers. However, most of them had also been worshiping Baal and Asherah. They had become polytheistic.

Asherah—The Goddess of Sex and War

Jezebel's father was a priest of Asherah, which explains her intense involvement in this pagan religion. The worship of this pagan god involved terrible licentiousness. This is why Jesus Christ in His letter to the church in Thyatira stated that these people—even as Christians—were tolerating "that woman Jezebel, who calls herself a prophetess. By her teaching," Jesus continued, "she misleads my servants into *sexual immorality* and the eating of food sacrificed to idols" (Rev. 2:20).

Baal—The Farm and Storm God

Knowing what Israel believed about Baal helps us understand why God wanted Elijah to confront Baal on Mount Carmel. Since they believed Baal was the "farm god," why had he allowed Israel to experience such a drought? Since he was also identified as Hadad—the storm god—why had he withheld rain from the earth? Israel actually believed that Baal's voice could be heard in the reverberating lightning and thunder that accompanied rain.

The picture is clear. God was about to demonstrate through Elijah that Baal was a fraud. More specifically, he didn't even exist. It also makes sense why God chose to judge Israel with a drought. The children of Israel were about to see that there was only one God who was in control of the elements—the God of Abraham, Isaac, and Jacob.

A Deafening Silence

When Elijah asked the children of Israel to make a choice between the Lord and Baal, their silence in itself "spoke loudly." They chose to say nothing (see 1 Kings 18:21b). Their response was a deafening stillness! But when they said "nothing," they revealed the thoughts and intents of their hearts.

The Israelites' Intentions

They didn't want to make a decision. Why choose? Why not worship both the God of their fathers as well as Baal? Why not include Asherah? Why be monotheistic? Couldn't they "have their cake and eat it too"? After all, isn't it being narrow-minded to believe there is only one God?

They were enjoying their worldly lifestyle. Let's face it! The moral codes of Jehovah were demanding and out of harmony with the "immoral codes" associated with pagan worship. The worship of Asherah particularly promoted all kinds of sexual immorality—including temple prostitution as a part of Israel's religious rituals. Both men and women have demonstrated over the years that it's a lot more fun to follow the desires of the flesh than the will of God—which condemns sexual promiscuity.

They were afraid to voice an opinion. We must remember that both King Ahab and Queen Jezebel worshiped these pagan gods. How would you feel at this moment? Ahab—who had called this public meeting in the first place—was standing beside Elijah when the old prophet asked Israel to make a choice between these false gods and the one true God.

Their silence is predictable. Even if they were inclined to worship and serve only the Lord God, it would take a great deal of courage and strong convictions to speak up for the one true God. It's not surprising that "the people said nothing."

Sodom and Gomorrah

Wavering between two opinions is not something new in biblical history—or in our own personal experiences. In the Old

Testament, what happened in Sodom and Gomorrah dramatically illustrates this tendency, even among God's people.

A Worldly Choice

Lot and his family chose to live in Sodom. They should not have made this choice in the first place—but they did. It was "sin city!" Sexual immorality was practiced openly in the streets. Imagine rearing your children in this environment!

As God normally does, He issued a stern warning to Lot and his family. After all, they were His children. However, Lot didn't want to leave—in spite of impending doom. But when he finally made the choice, the two angels God had sent to warn them "led them safely out of the city" (Gen. 19:16). But, had they not applied pressure, Lot and his family would have stayed in Sodom—ignoring God's warning of coming judgment.

"Don't Look Back!"

As soon as Lot and his family left the city, the two angels issued a stern warning: "Flee for your lives! Don't look back, and don't stop anywhere in the plain! Flee to the mountains or you will be swept away!" (v. 17).

Even then, "Lot's wife looked back." She ignored God's warning "and she became a pillar of salt" (v. 26). We're not told exactly what happened. Perhaps she lagged so far behind—not really wanting to leave "sin city"—that she was caught in a storm of burning sulphur that God rained down on these two evil cities. Perhaps God simply judged her for ignoring His warnings. Whatever the explanation, Lot's wife brought this calamity on herself because she—like the children of Israel on Mount Carmel—wavered "between two opinions." How enticing and deceptive sin can be!

"Choose This Day"

Joshua—Moses' successor and leader in Israel—was well aware of Israel's tendency to follow false gods. After they had eventually occupied the land of Canaan and before he "sent the people away, each to his own inheritance" (Josh. 24:28), he issued a solemn warning. In fact, it is in essence the same question Elijah posed to the people at Mount Carmel—only in the form of an exhortation. "Choose for yourselves this day whom you will serve, whether the gods your forefathers served beyond the River, or the gods of the Amorites, in whose land you are living. But as for me and my household, we will serve the LORD" (v. 15).

Even though the people responded positively and enthusiastically to Joshua's exhortation and personal witness, the next generation violated their parents' commitment. It's amazing how quickly it happened. Their parents had responded to Joshua's warning by saying, "Far be it from us to forsake the LORD to serve other gods" (v. 16). But we read that after Joshua's death, "another generation grew up . . . and served Baal and the Ashtoreths" (Judg. 2:10–13).

God's Marvelous Grace!

What is amazing is that this happened generation after generation in Israel. But what is even more amazing is that God—in His mercy and patience—reached out to His people again and again. This is what the Lord was doing through Elijah on Mount Carmel. Once again He was giving them another opportunity to follow Him—in spite of their persistent idolatry and immorality!

How often "the God of the Old Testament" is presented as a "God of wrath." At times, He certainly brought judgment. But in reality, we see God reflecting incredible patience and long-suffering. At the slightest response from His people in turning from their sins, He was quick to withdraw His judgments and to forgive them.

As stated, God at times judged Israel, but *always* after a very lengthy period of time when He issued warning after warning through His prophets. In the meantime, He tolerated some of the most horrible and hideous atrocities and crimes. Pagan worship not only involved gross immorality, but often involved taking the lives of innocent people. Child sacrifice was an intricate part of idolatry.

Becoming God's Man Today

Principles to Live By

Every Christian today must look carefully at what happened to the children of Israel generation after generation. How quickly they departed from the will of God and worshiped idols. How often they followed after their own fleshly desires. How easily they seemed to forget all that God had done for them. How hardened they became to the fact that they were bringing judgment, not only on themselves, but also on their children.

Elijah's question comes ringing and echoing down through the centuries as it rang out that day from Mount Carmel and echoed and reverberated through the canyons and out into the open valleys and plains at the foot of Mount Carmel: "How long will you waver between two opinions?"

Are You Double-Minded?

A double-minded Christian usually has one foot planted very firmly on the soil of this world's system and the other foot planted *very tentatively* in the soil of God's kingdom.

Double-minded Christians have not yet made the choice to follow Jesus Christ totally. Like Lot and his family, we've taken hold of God's hand but we are following half-heartedly. In our hearts, we "don't want to leave Sodom." Whether we acknowledge it or not, that's where we'd rather stay.

Some Christians respond like Lot's wife. They reluctantly "walk away" but keep "looking back."

A large number of Christians are like the children of Israel at Mount Carmel. When asked the question as to whom they are going to serve, they "say nothing." When this happens, their silence says it all!

Principle 1. Like the children of Israel, we don't want to make a decision.

Perhaps we're simply apathetic. The issue of whom we serve isn't that important to us. And who wants to be called a fanatic? "After all," we say, "there are many ways to heaven." To believe in "one way" is a sign of ignorance, cultural deprivation, and bigotry. So, why not "have our cake and eat it too!"

Principle 2. Like the children of Israel, we're enjoying our worldly lifestyle.

This is not surprising. In fact, this is the story of humanity. The Bible describes sin as attractive. Moses struggled with this decision for the same reasons we struggle. Thankfully, we read in Scripture that "he chose to be mistreated along with the people of God rather than to enjoy the pleasures of sin for a short time" (Heb. 11:25).

We often miss a very key phrase in this scriptural statement. The "pleasures of sin" are short-lived! They never satisfy. We go from one experience to another but we're never fulfilled.

All Are Tempted

Many times in my own life sin looks very attractive! It always does—and more so at a distance! The grass always seems greener on the other side of the fence, and at times I find myself wavering—stopping and looking both ways—and even moving in the wrong direction.

These feelings and desires should not surprise us. They are normal and natural. But when we yield, it leaves us feeling guilty, unsatisfied, and often brokenhearted. Ask any person who has yielded to Satan's subtle voice! Furthermore, read the Scriptures. They are filled with examples of people who failed God.

You need not experience the result of sin to be convinced that it's a dead-end street! To learn by personal experience is a horrible price to pay—especially when you don't have to. Ask David, or Saul, or Solomon!

Principle 3. Like the children of Israel,
we're afraid to take a stand.

For most of us, this may not be a serious problem. However, if you were a Muslim, you might be killed if you became a Christian. If you were from a strict Jewish home, you might be considered dead—and treated that way. And, if you were a part of some other religious group, you might be excommunicated.

A Personal Journey out of Double-Mindedness

I began this chapter by referring to my own religious background. For several years, I experienced a lot of double-minded moments in my life. Though my choices were not between the one true God and a false god, I experienced severe tension.

My parents were part of a very exclusive religious community. I grew up in this environment, going to Sunday School and church regularly as a child. At age sixteen, I made a very sincere decision and became an official member of the group. Though I already had reservations about some of the doctrinal teachings, I still believed it was probably *the best* of all religious communities.

After becoming a member of this group, I gradually began to see things differently. I became convinced that the leaders were teaching a number of doctrinal errors. Furthermore, I saw a lack of spiritual reality in the lives of many people. True, they were faithful church attenders, but their relationship with God and others was very inconsistent with what I was learning from the Scriptures.

My deep concerns created a deep desire to learn more about the Bible. Though it was forbidden, I began to attend Bible conferences sponsored by other Christian organizations. I also began to listen to a Christian radio station coming from Moody Bible Institute in Chicago. Through these experiences, I was motivated to study the Bible more on my own.

Toward the end of my high school years, I decided to attend Moody Bible Institute to learn more about the Bible. From the viewpoint of those in this religious group, this was my first major mistake. They disagreed vehemently with my decision. They didn't believe in formal Bible study. And to leave the group to study in a school of higher learning only intensified their concerns about me. Ironically, I became their "prodigal son."

My next "major mistake" was to marry a girl who was not a part of our religious community. Going to a school of higher education was one kind of sin, but to marry an "outsider" was an even greater departure from "the faith."

Strange as it may seem, the major issue was not whether or not to marry a Christian or a non-Christian. It was the fact that I was marrying someone who was not a part of this religious sect. According to my "spiritual leaders," no one outside of our religious community could possibly be acceptable to God.

What's the Big Deal?

To an outsider, the experience I just shared may seem to be a minor religious episode in the life of a young man. However, for me it was a very difficult process lasting for several years. I had been brought up in this religious community. My parents were a part of this environment. I had been indoctrinated in this religion and taught that we alone had religious truth. I had also been taught that to associate with other people who claimed to be Christians would definitely jeopardize my chances of ever inheriting eternal life. In fact, when I was excommunicated, those who took actions against me definitely believed I had departed from the faith and probably was hopelessly lost. In fact, many of them still believe this to be true today.

My Double-Mindedness Was Real

As a teenager, I was torn emotionally between what I had been taught and what I was learning from my study of Scripture. Though I saw definite contradictions, my cultural and emotional ties were overwhelming. They were at the root of my double-mindedness. To face the prospect of being rejected by those I had been taught to respect as God's human representatives on earth created a persistent fear—especially when I was around them. Furthermore, I had developed some very deep friendships.

The time finally came when I had to make a definite choice. In some respects, it was made for me. I was excommunicated because of what I believed and what I had done.

Once the decision was made, however, the chains that bound me fell off. Though it took time to heal emotionally, I immediately experienced a new sense of freedom. I stopped "wavering between two opinions." I now knew what I believed—and the most wonderful result of the whole process was to know that I was eternally saved. You see I had been taught from a child that you really can't be sure of eternal life until you pass into that "great beyond." Perhaps if I were good enough, attended church regularly, obeyed those who ruled over me, then God might smile on me and welcome me to heaven. This may help you understand why it was so difficult to take a stand against what I had been taught all those years.

Fear of Rejection

Are you afraid to make the right decision because you fear rejection? God understands that tension but He wants you to follow the truth. He wants you to make the right decision. Jesus Christ must be first in your life, not your cultural values.

Becoming a Man of Conviction

Perhaps you can identify with the children of Israel—or with my story.

> ➤ Are you wavering because you simply don't want to make a decision?

> ➤ Are you wavering because you are enjoying your worldly lifestyle?

> ➤ Are you wavering because you're afraid to take a stand?

As you evaluate your own life and the reasons for double-mindedness, pray and ask the Holy Spirit to impress on your heart why this is happening to you. Then write out a specific goal. For example, you may be enjoying a lifestyle that you know is out of harmony with the will of God. If so, perhaps the following prayer based on Scripture will help you:

Heavenly Father, today . . .

> ➤ I am going to serve only one Master, Jesus Christ the Lord (Matt. 6:24).

> ➤ I am going to continually seek first Your kingdom and Your righteousness (Matt. 6:33).

> ➤ I am going to deny myself and take up my cross daily and follow Jesus Christ (Mark 8:34).

> ➤ I now present my body to You and with Your help I will renew my mind daily in order to conform my life to Christ's will (Rom. 12:1–2).

Set a Goal

With God's help, I will begin immediately to carry out the following goal in my life:

_____

_____

_____

_____

Memorize the Following Scripture

If any of you lacks wisdom, he should ask God, who gives generously to all without finding fault, and it will be given to him. But when he asks, he must believe and not doubt, because he who doubts is like a wave of the sea, blown and tossed by the wind. That man should not think he will receive anything from the Lord; he is a double-minded man, unstable in all he does.

James 1:5–8

Chapter 8

Majesty—Not Magic!

Read 1 Kings 18:22–40

*M*y wife and I enjoy magic—realizing, of course, that it's all illusion! In fact, we had a very unusual encounter with David Copperfield—probably one of the greatest magicians since Houdini. At one point in his program, Copperfield came down from the platform and picked Elaine out of the audience. He had her stand dead center in the midst of a great crowd. He then took a paper napkin and carefully formed it into the shape of a rose. As good magicians do, he gave it to her so she could examine it, and then took it back. At that point, he let loose of it and it floated in thin air—over his arm, around his hand—all the time demonstrating there were no "strings attached"!

Copperfield then took a lighter from his pocket, ignited the "floating object," and the rose-shaped napkin burst into flames and disappeared. At that moment, from out of nowhere, Copperfield reached up and grabbed a real rose floating in front of him and, in the midst of great applause, handed it to my wife as a gift.

"How did he do that?" everyone was asking themselves—including my wife and me. Yes, it was real! I held it and smelled it when she came back and sat down.

It was, of course, an illusion! In fact, it was a minor trick compared with the other incredible things David Copperfield did that evening.

True magicians, of course, admit openly that what they do has nothing to do with the supernatural. They simply have learned the fantastic art of "deceiving us" in various ways! And it's fun.

No Illusion!

When King Ahab and the prophets of Baal and all of Israel met Elijah on top of Mount Carmel, it was not to have fun! Neither were they about to see an illusion. Elijah was not a magician. He was a man of God who was going to be used by God to unleash one of the greatest demonstrations of supernatural power since the time Moses stretched out his rod and God parted the Red Sea!

Where Was Jezebel?

Initially, Elijah challenged "the four hundred and fifty prophets of Baal" as well as "the four hundred prophets of Asherah" (1 Kings 18:19). Ahab accepted the challenge—but only the prophets of Baal responded to his command. We're not told why, but we can speculate. Personally, I think Jezebel simply ignored Elijah's challenge and told Ahab in no uncertain terms that she and her prophets were not going to accommodate this prophet. Knowing her character, she probably felt it would be condescending.

Perhaps Ahab thought this was his great opportunity to prove to himself and to all Israel that he *could do something* without Jezebel. Had he known what was about to happen, he would have ignored Elijah too. Little did he realize that he would soon return and have to face his queen with a story of embarrassing defeat (see 19:1).

Setting the Stage

When the people of Israel gathered at Mount Carmel, Elijah issued his challenge: "How long will you waver between two opinions? If the LORD is God, follow him; but if Baal is God, follow him" (18:21).

As we've seen in our previous chapter, there was a deafening silence. The people refused to choose, which was in reality a choice—a choice to continue in their pagan practices.

This didn't catch Elijah off guard. He knew their hearts. But he had "set the stage" for the Lord to demonstrate that He was the One true God.

Four Hundred and Fifty to One

It was not an accident that Elijah pointed out the great disparity in this contest. It was he alone—a prophet of God—who was about to do battle with four hundred and fifty prophets of Baal (see v. 22). This was all a part of God's plan to demonstrate His power. Elijah purposely didn't ask for a single representative from the prophets (which was normally done in this kind of duel or contest). Elijah wanted the people to see the enormity of this comparison. In fact, he was hoping to include the prophets of Asherah in this contest—which would have made it eight hundred and fifty to one.

Elijah proceeded with his plan as if this were a one-to-one battle. "Get two bulls for us," he told the people (v. 23). Again, we see Elijah's wisdom. Since the people chose the bulls, they couldn't accuse him of dishonesty or some form of trickery. He even gave the prophets of Baal first choice, eliminating the possibility of being accused later of having some underhanded scheme (see v. 25).

The Ground Rules

To make sure there were no misunderstandings, Elijah very specifically outlined the ground rules. Once they chose the bull they wanted for the sacrifice, the prophets of Baal were to cut the bull into pieces and lay it on a pile of wood. However, they were *not* to set the sacrifice on fire. Elijah agreed to do the same. Rather, both sides were to call on their respective "gods"—they on Baal and he on the name of the Lord—and, "the god who answers by fire," Elijah proposed, "he is God" (v. 24).

At this point the people broke their silence. "What you say is good," they responded (v. 24b). In actuality, they had no choice. Elijah's proposal was more than fair. To reject it would be to admit that they were afraid to pit Baal and the 450 prophets against the Lord God and His lone representative.

Another Opportunity to Upstage Him!

Once the children of Israel approved his plan, Elijah focused on the prophets. Once again, he gave them the edge. In fact, he gave them every opportunity to upstage him. "Choose one of the bulls and prepare it first," he said. Don't miss the sarcasm in his voice as he finished his statement—"Prepare it first," he quipped, *"since there are so many of you"* (v. 25).

Even if Elijah's sarcasm made them angry, they couldn't refuse his offer. They'd be admitting defeat before the contest began. They knew—and so did all Israel—that Elijah's proposal was heavily stacked in their favor. If they had made any alternate suggestions, it would have weakened their credibility in the eyes of the people.

Elijah's faith and sense of security in this situation must have also unnerved these false prophets. But they couldn't turn back, even if they sensed they were headed for trouble. Their position of power was at stake. More importantly, they were under orders from King Ahab!

Futile Prayers

Imagine the scene. Four hundred and fifty men "called on the name of Baal from morning till noon" (v. 26). They shouted at the top of their voices! They danced feverishly! Later in the day, they became so frustrated that they "slashed themselves with swords . . . until their blood flowed" (v. 28). All day long they cried out to Baal! We read that "they continued their frantic prophesying until the time for the evening sacrifice" (v. 29).

The children of Israel waited expectantly—no doubt growing restless as the day wore on. The heavens matched their own silence when they had refused to respond to Elijah's initial challenge. Baal—who supposedly was in charge of the weather—did not respond. There was no thunder, no lightning, no fire! We simply read that "there was no response, no one answered, no one paid attention" (v. 29). But for Elijah, it was an electrifying moment!

Elijah's Biting Sarcasm

Initially, Elijah stood by silently. However, by noontime he could restrain himself no longer. He began to taunt the prophets of Baal. "Shout louder!" he said. "Surely he is a god! Perhaps he is deep in thought, or busy, or traveling. Maybe he is sleeping and must be awakened" (v. 27).

Elijah understood the theology of Baalism. When their prayers failed, the pagan prophets told the people that Baal at times was "deep in thought," or that in some instances he had "taken a journey" and hadn't returned, or that he was "sleeping and needed to be awakened." Elijah used the opportunity to contrast what they actually believed with what was actually happening. If Baal was the god they thought he was, why hadn't he responded to all of this frantic noise and motion? After all, there were four hundred and fifty men shouting and dancing! How could *any* god sleep through that?

The Plan Worked!

Don't misunderstand. Elijah didn't intend for his sarcasm to be a display of pride and arrogance. Rather, he was teaching Israel an important lesson. His strategy worked. Once Elijah challenged them, they "shouted louder!" They even injured themselves. They knew their lives were at stake. If Elijah won this battle, they would be in deep trouble not only with King Ahab but with all of Israel.

The prophets of Baal also knew how cruel Jezebel could be! If they failed, she would find out about it within hours. She certainly must have had her spies watching this incredible event. Imagine her response when she received word that the prophets of Baal had continued their pagan ritual all day long "until the time for the evening sacrifice" (v. 29), and nothing had happened! There were no clouds in the sky. There was no thunder, no lightning bolts, no fire from heaven. She must have been throwing her own temper tantrum!

This Was Elijah's Moment!

The time had come! The prophets of Baal had failed miserably. This was the moment Elijah had been waiting for. All eyes were on him. You see, *God's plan* was right on schedule. Had Elijah gone first, the battle would have been over before it was started. There would have been no backdrop against which to demonstrate God's mighty power—a backdrop of total and utter failure on the part of these pagan prophets. But now, the stage was finally set! What a teachable moment!

Elijah saw this as a great opportunity. He took his time and asked the people to gather around and watch what he was doing. First, "he repaired the altar of the LORD, which was in ruins" (v. 30). Later, we discover why. Israel no longer worshiped God. They had destroyed the altars that were once used to praise and honor the God of heaven (see 19:10,14).

"Don't You Remember?"

Elijah rebuilt the altar with "twelve stones, one for each of the tribes" that had "descended from Jacob" (18:31). He was reminding the watching multitudes of their sacred history. We're not told that Elijah said anything while he was rebuilding the altar, but it's difficult to imagine that he worked in silence. As he put each stone in place, he must have recounted

God's marvelous grace in calling Israel out of Egypt and giving them an inheritance in Canaan.

Let's use our "sanctified imagination!" Elijah may have recounted the Lord's instructions to Joshua after Israel had crossed Jordan miraculously. As Elijah put each stone in place, his conversation may have gone something like this: "Don't you remember what God did for our forefathers at the Jordan River? Don't you remember how He backed up the water as our people crossed over into Canaan on dry ground? And don't you remember what God told Joshua? He was to choose twelve men from among the people—one from each tribe. Furthermore, God told our forefather, Joshua, to have these men He had chosen to take up twelve stones from the middle of the Jordan. And when they moved on to Gilgal, they set up these stones as a memorial to the Lord."

"Do you know why God issued these instructions?" Elijah may have asked—as he put another stone in place. "Let me tell you!" At this point, Elijah may have quoted Joshua:

> "In the future when your descendants ask their fathers, 'What do these stones mean?' tell them, 'Israel crossed the Jordan on dry ground. For the LORD your God dried up the Jordan before you until you had crossed over. The LORD your God did to the Jordan just what he had done to the Red Sea when he dried it up before us until we had crossed over. He did this so that all the peoples of the earth might know that the hand of the LORD is powerful and so that you might always fear the LORD your God.'" (Josh. 4:21–24)

Though only a small number in the great multitude gathered at Mount Carmel would be able to see and hear what Elijah may have said, they would have passed the word from person to person down through the valleys and out into the plains—which is all the more reason why Elijah would take his time.

This Was No Illusion!

Elijah next move was very dramatic! To make sure that Israel knew what was about to happen was no trick, Elijah "dug a trench" around the altar (1 Kings 18:32). He then prepared the sacrifice, but he asked the people themselves to pour water on the altar. He had them fill "four large jars with water" three times and then pour the water all over the offering and on the wood (see v. 33). In fact, they poured so much water on the sacrifice that it actually filled the trench at the base of the altar (see v. 35).

Elijah wanted the people to know beyond a shadow of a doubt that what was about to happen was a miracle—not a trick. There was no way there could have been a "secret" fire burning under the altar. No one could accuse Elijah of using sleight of hand to start the fire himself. The wood was soaked and so was the meat. There was no way it could suddenly ignite. The people were about to see God's majesty!

Seconds . . . and Counting!

Elijah's plan coincided with the "time of sacrifice." At that moment he "stepped forward and prayed." He didn't shout! He didn't dance! And he didn't cut himself! And as far as we know, he repeated the prayer only once. All in all, it took only a few seconds to say what he had to say: "O LORD, God of Abraham, Isaac and Israel, let it be known today that *you are God* in Israel and that *I am your servant* and have done all these things *at your command*. Answer me, O LORD, answer me, so these people will know that you, O LORD, are God, and that you are *turning their hearts* back again" (vv. 36–37). Note four important elements in Elijah's prayer:

"You Are God"

Elijah made it crystal clear in his prayer that the purpose behind what was about to happen was to demonstrate that *the Lord was God*.

"I Am Your Servant"

Elijah also wanted everyone to know beyond a shadow of a doubt that he was merely a human agent *serving God*.

"At Your Command"

Furthermore, Elijah wanted Israel to know that what he was doing was not of his own making. It was not to demonstrate his power, but God's power. The Lord had spoken to him and the dramatic things that he had said and that they were about to see were a result of God's command.

"Turning Their Hearts"

Most importantly, Elijah wanted Israel to know that the major reason God was about to demonstrate His power was to turn their hearts back to Him. He was reaching out to them. He was demonstrating mercy, as He had done so many times before. He was faithfully keeping His promises to His faithless people.

Irrefutable Proof

There is one thing that is clear in Scripture. When God wants people to know that He is speaking directly from heaven, He is far from subtle. His message is always clear. And so it was on Mount Carmel. He indeed offered irrefutable proof. Though the human stage had been set with twelve stones, the wood, a sacrifice—all drenched with water—God was now to add the divine dimension. In an instance, the "fire of the LORD fell and burned up the sacrifice" and "the wood." But the fire of God burned up not only the water-soaked logs, but "the stones and the soil and also licked up the water in the trench" (v. 38). The children of Israel were witnessing the awesome power of God!

Imagine the horror that must have been reflected in the faces of every observer. Fire that hot would have driven them back and away from the altar that no longer existed. Furthermore, there was a powerful message in this display of power—one they could not miss. In destroying the twelve stones, symbolic of the twelve tribes, God was saying that He was capable of destroying all Israel! Once again, God was warning His people of what would eventually happen if they continued to reject His love and mercy. But, more importantly, at this moment His message of judgment was also his message of love. He was giving them another opportunity to turn from their idolatry and sin and once again follow Him.

"The Lord, He Is God!"

God's message was loud and clear to Israel. They fell prostrate on the ground and cried, "The Lord, he is God! The Lord— he is God!" (1 Kings 18:39). Those closest probably began the chant and those farther out joined them in the ever-widening circle of people shouting, "The Lord, he is God!" How long they repeated this proclamation, we're not told.

What a sight this must have been! And what a verbal message! It must have reverberated through the valley for miles.

The prophets of Baal shouted for hours asking Baal for *proof* that he was a god. The children of Israel were shouting a proclamation that the Lord *was* God! They had their proof!

"The Wages of Sin Is Death"

God not only proved that He was God by sending fire from heaven, but His judgment fell on the prophets of Baal. At Elijah's command, the people themselves seized these evil men and executed them in the Kishon Valley (see v. 40).

There is also a message for all humanity in this tragic event in the lives of these false prophets. God's judgment will eventually fall on all those who deny Him. Though His mercy is great and His long-suffering beyond measure, there will come a day when unbelievers will be separated from God forever. The Scriptures teach that "the wages of sin is death" (Rom. 6:23). There will come a day when all people who deny God and His Son, Jesus Christ, will be eternally punished and separated from God's presence (see Rev. 20:7–14).

On the other hand, the Bible teaches that those who respond to God's love and grace will be saved. The same Scripture that teaches that "the wages of sin is death," also teaches that "the gift of God is eternal life through Jesus Christ our Lord" (Rom. 6:23).

God Is Love

There's one major truth that emerges from this dramatic Mount Carmel experience. God was reaching out in love to Israel. He wanted them to know that He was God and that He was their Source of life, both temporal and eternal. Elijah's prayer focuses this great truth (see 1 Kings 18:37).

"I Am . . . the Truth!"

This is in essence the Truth that emerges from the whole of Scripture. God wants to turn all of our hearts back to Him. It's the main story line that flows through the Bible from Genesis to Revelation. The moment Adam and Eve sinned and became spiritually separated from God, the Lord began to reach out to them and to all people with a plan of restoration (see Gen. 3:15; 12:1–3). The children of Israel—all through history—have been a unique part of that plan. Today, Jesus Christ—the "promised seed"—is crying out, "I am the way, the truth and the life" (John 14:6).

Mountaintop Experiences

To understand the real significance of what happened between Elijah and the prophets of Baal on Mount Carmel, we need to look at two additional mountaintop experiences, all associated with three main time periods in biblical history when God revealed Himself to humans directly and in a very dramatic way. The first involved Moses; the second, Elijah; and the third, Jesus Christ. God's first major revelation, combining who He was and what His will is for His people, happened on *Mount Sinai.* His second revelation was on *Mount Carmel.*

And His third revelation was on what has come to be called the *mount of transfiguration.*

Mount Sinai

When God used Moses to lead the children of Israel out of Egypt, He eventually brought them to Mount Sinai. It was there that—for the first time—He revealed His moral laws which are spelled out in the Ten Commandments. However, this revelation did not involve only words. God confirmed this message with "signs" and "wonders" and "miracles."

The Book of Exodus has described these events in detail:

> On the morning of the third day there was thunder and lightning, with a thick cloud over the mountain, and a very loud trumpet blast. Everyone in the camp trembled. . . . Mount Sinai was covered with smoke, because the LORD descended on it in fire. The smoke billowed up from it like smoke from a furnace, the whole mountain trembled violently, and the sound of the trumpet grew louder and louder." (Exod. 19:16,18–19)

It was in the midst of this glorious and awesome demonstration of God's power that "Moses spoke" to God and "God answered him." It was also during this dramatic demonstration that God "called Moses to the top of the mountain" and revealed His laws to Israel (v. 20).

One thing is very clear! God wanted Israel—and us—to know for sure it was He who was speaking, not a "false god." Consequently, the Lord verified His message with a never-to-be-forgotten demonstration of His power.

Mount Carmel

Against the backdrop of this "fireworks" display at Mount Sinai, we can more easily grasp what took place on Mount Carmel. Once again God was speaking! However, this time He was attempting to turn Israel's hearts back to His will and ways. They had departed from His laws, had forsaken Him, and turned to Baal, a false god, who had no divine power whatsoever. And once again, God did not leave question marks in Israel's mind regarding who He was. He had already revealed His laws at Mount Sinai. At this point, the Lord was calling them back to obedience, but verifying once again with His supernatural power that He was indeed the almighty and living God.

The Mount of Transfiguration

The third great event marking God's efforts at reaching out to Israel, as well as to the whole world, involved His Son, Jesus Christ. This was indeed His greatest revelation of all! Though Christ's birth, life, miracles—and all that He did and said— are involved in this revelation, His primary purpose in coming to earth is beautifully and powerfully illustrated on another mountaintop—the mount of transfiguration.

One day Jesus Christ ascended a mountain to pray, taking with Him three well-known apostles—Peter, James, and John. While Christ was talking with His heavenly Father, "the appearance of his face changed, and his clothes became as bright as a flash of lightning" (Luke 9:29). Not coinciden- tally—especially in view of what happened on Mount Sinai and on Mount Carmel— *"Moses and Elijah,* appeared in glori- ous splendor, talking with Jesus" (vv. 30–31).

The disciples were dumbfounded! While Peter was verbally stumbling around trying to say something appropriate, "a cloud appeared and enveloped them" and "a voice came from the cloud, saying, 'This is my Son, whom I have chosen; listen to him'" (vv. 34–35).

"In These Last Days"

This supernatural event symbolized God's great and final reve- lation of Himself before Christ will come again, first to take all believers home to heaven, and then to set up His kingdom on earth, leading to the great and final judgment.

This is one of the primary messages in the Book of Hebrews:

In the past God spoke to our forefathers through the prophets at many times and in various ways, but *in these last days he has spoken to us by his Son,* whom he appointed heir of all things, and through whom he made the universe. The Son is the radiance of God's glory and the exact representation of his being, sustaining all things by his powerful word. After he had provided purification for sins, he sat down at the right hand of the Majesty in heaven." (Heb. 1:1–3)

A few paragraphs later, the author of Hebrews issues a sobering warning:

We must pay more careful attention, therefore, to what we have heard. . . . How shall we escape if we ignore such a great salvation? This salvation, which was first announced by the Lord, was confirmed to us by those who heard him. God also testified to it by signs, wonders and various miracles, and gifts of the Holy Spirit distributed according to his will. (2:1–4)

Have You Heard God's Message?

God does not reveal Himself in subtle ways:

➤ At Mount Sinai He appeared in the context of lightning and thunder, fire and smoke, and a quaking mountain.

➤ At Mount Carmel He appeared in the fire that fell from heaven and destroyed not only the offering but the altar and the water in the trench.

➤ And when God revealed Himself through Jesus Christ and the apostles, He did so in the context of "signs, wonders and various miracles, and gifts of the Holy Spirit" (Heb. 2:4)—turning water to wine, walking on the water, calming the storm, healing blind people, casting out demons, and raising the dead. For all those who were willing to listen to Christ and the apostles, there is no question but that God was—and is—speaking.

Powerful Moments in History

These three major events covered a total time span lasting approximately one hundred and fifty years. They represent the "powerful moments" in history when God revealed Himself in a special way, and verified His majesty, His power, and His glory. Within "these moments," God revealed very specifically His message of salvation and redemption. Again, have you heard this message? More importantly, have you accepted this message?

The "Silent Years"

Some have defined the rest of history—literally thousands of years—as periods known as God's "silent years." This does not mean that God has not been present nor active in the affairs of mankind! For Christians, He dwells in our hearts and continues to reveal His power to enable us to "be filled to the measure of all the fullness of God" (see Eph. 3:14–19). But generally speaking, God has not been speaking directly to men and women, accompanying His message with signs and wonders as He did through Moses, Elijah, and Elisha, and Christ and the apostles. In fact, nearly two thousand years have passed since God's last great revelation through His Son. If the author of Hebrews is correct—and we believe he is—there will be no major manifestations of this nature until Jesus Christ comes again.

Please don't misunderstand. This does not mean that God cannot—and does not—work miracles today. This does not mean He is unconcerned about His children. This does not mean that He doesn't answer prayer in powerful ways. Rather, it simply means that His method of communicating with us today is far more subtle than it was during these great and awesome "moments" in history. Some well-meaning people have tried to duplicate "these great moments," and when they do, it has always led to all kinds of bizarre and confusing experiences.

Becoming God's Man Today

Principles to Live By

Principle 1. God is speaking through the Scriptures. Have you heard His voice?

Don't wait for some "sign" or unique manifestation. Again, the author of Hebrews speaks with urgency: "Today, if you hear his voice, do not harden your hearts" (Heb. 3:15).

This message is for both Christians and non-Christians. If you are a believer walking out of the will of God, confess your sins and accept forgiveness and once again enjoy fellowship with the Lord (see 1 John 1:9). If you are an unbeliever, receive Jesus Christ today. He died for you and was resurrected so you might have eternal life. Receive the free gift of salvation (see John 1:12).

Principle 2. God is long-suffering and patient.

How true this was in God's dealings with Israel! It's still true today.

I personally believe that the next major dramatic event will be when Jesus Christ comes again. When He comes, even those who have rejected God and His Son will bow the knee to Jesus Christ. Paul tells us that every tongue will "confess that Jesus Christ is Lord" (Phil. 2:11). Unfortunately, for many it will be too late to inherit eternal life, for they will bow out of force rather than out of freedom. They, along with Satan and his evil demons, will have to acknowledge that God is God! Satan, of course, acknowledges that even now—but he certainly has not bowed the knee.

Principle 3. We're still living in God's day of grace.

God is still offering an invitation for salvation. We still have access to His long-suffering and mercy. In fact, Peter reminds us that He has not returned to judge the earth because "He is patient . . . not wanting anyone to perish, but everyone to come to repentance. But," Peter continues, "the day of the Lord *will come* like a thief. The heavens will disappear with a roar; the elements will be destroyed by fire, and the earth and everything in it will be laid bare" (2 Pet. 3:9–10).

Becoming a Man Who Follows God

The very week I was preparing this material, I received a call around midnight. I'd already retired. It was an executive with a well-known corporation. One of their employees was a man in my church who traveled extensively to foreign countries. While doing business in Singapore, he died of a heart attack, and the executive had called to ask me to help communicate his death to his wife and family.

Fortunately, Rick was ready to meet the Lord. He was a devoted Christian—a wonderful husband and father. But, he wasn't an old man—he was in his forties. Furthermore, he was in great shape physically. He had just passed a physical with flying colors. The week before he had run a 5-K race. He had no history of a heart condition. There was no human reason for him to die—but he did! Fortunately, he was ready to meet the Lord Jesus Christ. Are you?

Is it possible that you may be taking advantage of God's long-suffering and patience? Ask yourself these questions.

➤ Do I read the Scriptures regularly to determine God's will for my life?

➤ Do I understand God's long-suffering and patience with me—and all of humanity?

➤ Am I ready to meet Jesus Christ when He comes—or when I die?

Set a Goal

With God's help, I will begin immediately to carry out the following goal in my life:

_____

_____

_____

_____

Memorize the Following Scripture

Today, if you hear his voice, do not harden your hearts.

HEBREWS 3:7–8, 15; 4:7

Chapter 9

Overcoming Depression
Read 1 Kings 18:41–46; 19:1–9

I recently received a call from a successful businessman. "Gene," he said—with a note of desperation in his voice—"I'm in deep trouble. I feel as if I'm living with a heavy, wet blanket over my head. I can hardly breathe. I don't want to get up and face the day's activities. My motivation is at an all-time low. I can't even think clearly. I'm feeling immobilized. I can't even function properly in my business."

It didn't take long to discern that my friend was terribly depressed. Knowing the struggles he'd gone through over the past several years, I wasn't surprised. Because of my close relationship to people at the Minirth-Meier New Life Clinic in Dallas, I was able to get him an appointment with a good Christian counselor. The diagnosis was what I had anticipated. My friend was plagued with chemical depression—an imbalance of our body's own chemicals, brought on by extreme stress.

The good news is that he responded quickly to medication and counseling—and was able to once again cope with the challenges he faced in life. It also helped him to establish some new spiritual goals.

A Common Human Experience

All Christians face times of depression—even some of God's choicest servants. Elijah certainly demonstrates this reality. What may be surprising is that Elijah's bout with depression came after his greatest spiritual victory. It happened suddenly and seemingly without warning. But in retrospect, it was predictable.

An Emotional High

Following Elijah's great spiritual victory on Mount Carmel, he had great hopes for revival in Israel. Understandably so! The people responded en masse and acknowledged that the Lord was the one true God (see 1 Kings 18:39). Their punitive actions against the prophets of Baal also indicated their desire to turn from their idolatrous ways (see v. 40).

Ahab's response encouraged Elijah the most. The king's heart appeared soft and humble before the Lord. Following his utter defeat, Ahab's countenance must have reflected horrible dejection and weariness.

Rather than condemning the king, Elijah encouraged him to return to his royal tent and regain his emotional and physical strength. "Go, eat and drink," Elijah said, "for there is the sound of a heavy rain" (v. 41). In other words, Elijah was telling Ahab to cheer up! The drought was over.

What Elijah actually "heard" at that moment was in his heart. With the "ear of faith" he knew rain was on its way, even though there were no visible clouds, no thunder, and no lightning. But Elijah knew there would be! His knowledge of God's will enabled him to "hear" things others couldn't hear. God had spoken, and the fire from heaven was just the beginning of what God had promised would happen.

As Ahab "went off to eat and drink," Elijah once again made his way to the top of Mount Carmel to pray and wait for God to send rain. From that vantage point, he and his servant could look over the vast expanse of the Mediterranean.

Elijah instructed his servants seven times to climb to a look-out point to see if there was any evidence of the coming storm. The seventh time, the servant returned with a positive report. He had seen "a cloud as small as a man's hand . . . rising from the sea" (v. 44).

This was all the visible evidence Elijah needed. He told Ahab to get his chariot ready and to head for Jezreel before the rain became so intense it would be impossible to travel (see v. 44). Suddenly, "the sky grew black with clouds, the wind rose," and "a heavy rain" began to fall (v. 45).

Elijah's Marathon

As "Ahab rode off to Jezreel" in the blinding rainstorm, a strange thing happened! "The power of the LORD came upon Elijah" and he tucked "his cloak into his belt" and "ran ahead of Ahab all the way to Jezreel" (v. 46).

Where Was Ahab's Runner?

Ahab's security team had probably vanished. A key member of that team was Ahab's personal runner—a man who ran out ahead of his chariot to make sure the road was clear. In light of the shocking events that had just transpired on Mount Carmel as well as the mass execution of the prophets of Baal, it's understandable why the designated runner went into hiding.

Imagine Ahab's surprise when Elijah suddenly became a part of his security team. Though the king could barely see through the blinding storm, he no doubt caught glimpses of Elijah—head bowed low and his cloak flapping in the wind as he braved the elements and led the king's chariot over winding, muddy roads back to Jezreel.

An Impossible Feat

Keep in mind that the distance from Mount Carmel to Jezreel—where Ahab had his summer palace—was nearly twenty miles. In view of Elijah's age, this was an impossible feat for an old man. The Lord had suddenly shifted His presence and power to Elijah, not to harm Ahab, but to help him! This must have been very reassuring to Ahab at this moment in his life.

Imagine Facing Jezebel

Another reason the Lord enabled Elijah to run ahead of Ahab's chariot relates to what the king would face when he returned to his palace. Jezebel would be waiting! Ahab would need all the emotional support he could get to stand up to this wicked woman and her four hundred prophets.

A Devastating Disappointment

Things did not turn out as Elijah had anticipated. His hopes were dashed. When Ahab reported on the Mount Carmel experience, Jezebel was livid (see 1 Kings 19:1–2)! Ahab—weak man that he was—would not stand up to his wicked queen.

Imagine how Elijah felt when he received the following message from Jezebel: "May the gods deal with me, be it ever so severely, if by this time tomorrow I do not make your life like that of one of them" (v. 2).

Elijah was hoping for a positive report that Jezebel had listened to Ahab, and had humbled herself before Almighty God. But not so! Like the pharaoh of Egypt, she hardened her heart. She only became more entrenched in her pagan ways and more steeped in her idolatry. Flying into a rage, she threatened to kill Elijah!

In the midst of her intense anger, Jezebel did not lose complete rationality. To unleash her fury on Elijah would put her own life in danger. She knew that the children of Israel had responded positively to what had happened on Mount Carmel. She was well aware of what they had done to the four hundred and fifty prophets of Baal. Emotions were running high. Consequently, she knew she had to give Elijah a way out. This is why she gave him twenty-four hours to get out of town!

Depression Strikes

When Elijah received Jezebel's message, there was an incredible change in his personality. His joy turned to sadness and his boldness to fear. He "was afraid" of Jezebel's threats and "ran for his life" (v. 3).

"Take My Life!"

After facing four hundred and fifty prophets of Baal so victoriously, Elijah was now running from Jezebel! Wasn't God able to protect him from this evil woman? Clearly, Elijah had lost perspective and entered a state of deep depression. In some respects, this should not surprise us since Elijah *was* "a man just like us." The King James translation is even more literal and accurate. We read that he "was a man subject to like passions [of like feelings] as we are" (James 5:17).

Elijah's depression was so severe that he wanted to die. In fact, he actually *"prayed* that he might die." Pouring out his soul before God, he cried out, "I have had enough, LORD. . . . Take my life" (1 Kings 19:4).

God Understood

In a state of emotional depression and physical exhaustion, Elijah laid down under a tree in the wilderness and fell sound asleep (v. 5). We're not told how long he slept, but suddenly, an angel of the Lord awakened him and told him to "get up and eat." To Elijah's amazement, "there by his head was a cake of bread baked over hot coals, and a jar of water" (v. 6). God had not forsaken His servant.

Though Elijah's depression was severe, it didn't affect his appetite. "He ate and drank and then lay down again." As before, we're not told how long he slept but eventually the angel returned and awakened him the second time and gave him the same instructions and once again, Elijah dined under a broom tree in the wilderness.

Little by little Elijah gained his physical strength. However, it would take more than food and rest to bring emotional healing to Elijah's soul. Though his pace was slow, we read that "he traveled forty days and forty nights until he reached Horeb, the mountain of God." There he found a cave and entered and "spent the night" (v. 8–9).

Explanations for Elijah's Depression

Depression often follows "mountaintop experiences." Elijah's experiences illustrates this point both symbolically and literally. Ironically, his "emotional highs" took place on the top of Mount Carmel. Imagine the excitement and joy that must have flooded his soul when God responded to his prayers and sent fire from heaven. For three and a half years he had been waiting for this moment. Like all of us, when Elijah experienced this incredible emotional high, he was also destined to experience an intense emotional low. It's a predictable pattern in human behavior.

Depression often follows intense periods of stress and hyperactivity. Though Elijah's emotions had to have peaked on Mount Carmel, remember that he also experienced unusual stress as he confronted the prophets of Baal. Though he certainly knew in his heart that God would answer his prayers, at the same time he experienced all of the physiological effects that accompany this kind of emotional wear and tear. Adrenalin was pouring into his bloodstream—and although the Lord had granted him unusual strength in running a twenty-mile "marathon" in a blinding rainstorm, Elijah was also drawing on his normal and natural resources.

All of us have a physical alarm system that is activated under stress. It's this system that provides us with unusual strength to go without sleep, to accomplish what appear to be superhuman tasks, and to concentrate beyond our normal abilities. But once these activities are over, our alarm system "turns off" and everything returns to normal. When this happens, depression is predictable. All of these dynamics contributed to Elijah's sudden personality change—even though his burst of energy enabling him to run twenty miles was definitely supernatural.

Depression often coincides with physical and emotional exhaustion. God has created each one of us to function within certain physiological and psychological boundaries. When we extend our energy outside these boundaries over a prolonged period, we are going to suffer the consequences. Unless we recreate and recuperate, we'll not rebound properly.

It's easy to conclude that Elijah had stretched himself far beyond any human being's normal physical and emotional boundaries. His stressful experience on Mount Carmel and his twenty-mile run had left him exhausted. Jezebel's threat became the "straw that broke the camel's back"! This helps explain why he ran from the problem. From a human point of view, he could no longer handle what he was ordinarily able to cope with emotionally.

Another mark that characterized Elijah's depression was his psychological distortions. The facts are that Jezebel's threats were minor compared with what had happened on Mount Carmel. Normally, Elijah would have been able to also discern that Jezebel's threats reflected her own fear. Why couldn't he just believe that God could protect him from this wicked woman? The answer to this question is obvious. He was terribly depressed!

Depression often follows keen disappointment and disillusionment. Elijah had high hopes for national repentance in Israel. He was excited about Ahab's initial response on Mount Carmel. In fact, he did all he could to forge ahead through this crisis. He even became his servant and ran ahead of the king's chariot all the way back to the palace. No doubt he truly believed that Ahab would take charge once he returned to Jezreel and dealt with Jezebel's idolatrous behavior.

But it didn't happen! All that Elijah had hoped for was dashed! His disappointment quickly turned into disillusionment. In the midst of his physical and emotional exhaustion, he dropped over the edge both spiritually and psychologically.

Depression often results from periods of anger, particularly if we don't deal with it properly. It's difficult to discern how much of Elijah's depression related to feelings of anger. It's not difficult, however, to understand that anger would be a natural emotion in this set of circumstances. After all, he had given himself totally to vindicate God's name. He had done his best to encourage Ahab to take a similar stand for righteousness. And as we've seen, he had high hopes for Israel. But he also knew that there would be no significant and permanent changes in the children of Israel if the king himself did not change.

The one factor that is missing in Elijah's experience is that he didn't have time to brood—to "let the sun go down" while he was "still angry" (Eph. 4:26). Excitement suddenly turned to sadness and despair. This may explain why he responded so quickly to God's plan for healing.

On the other hand, we must remind ourselves again that Elijah was "a man just like us." He had endured a great deal of difficulty for three and a half years. It would not be surprising if he had experienced some pretty severe bouts with anger—perhaps repressing those feelings. This, of course, is pure speculation. But the fact remains that we know that "repressed anger" does contribute significantly to depression. In fact, it is a very predictable emotional dynamic.

Becoming God's Man Today

Principles to Live By

Principle 1. Being a dedicated Christian who is used of God in significant ways does not guarantee that we'll not experience depression.

Like Elijah, we're all human. We have our physical and psychological limits. If we violate these limits on a prolonged basis, we'll experience the consequences.

This does not mean that we are necessarily unspiritual. Furthermore, it does not mean that we are necessarily out of the will of God when we violate these limits. In fact, the normal demands of life often force us into these situations. Making a living, academic pursuits, parenting, and other domestic responsibilities often push us beyond our normal boundaries. And, of course, ministry responsibilities are even more demanding. This is why God created us with these "alarm systems."

The important principle to remember is that depression does not necessarily mean that we are out of fellowship with God. Simply understanding this truth will enable us to deal with depression and overcome it without intensifying the problem by feeling guilty.

Principle 2. Under certain circumstances, Christians should expect to experience depression and its accompanying results.

When we face "mountaintop experiences" emotionally, and when we find ourselves in the midst of intense periods of stress and hyperactivity, we should be prepared to face the consequences. Eventually—if we're human at all—we'll face low points emotionally. This is very predictable when we've used up our physical and emotional reserves.

Remember, too, that disillusionment and disappointment cause depression. Since these factors are a very common part of life, we should not be surprised and caught off guard when we get depressed. It's normal to experience periodic low points.

Principle 3. Depression always distorts our view of reality.

Elijah lost mental and emotional perspective when Jezebel threatened his life. Though he could certainly recall the specific events that happened on Mount Carmel, he had difficulty remembering "emotionally." In fact, in the midst of his fear that was generated by Jezebel's threats, he even had difficulty remembering God's faithfulness in the past. God's supernatural provisions in the Kerith Ravine and in the home of the widow were beyond his psychological reach.

This should not surprise us. Depression thwarts our emotional memories and blurs our view of reality. God's acts of faithfulness in the past tend to lose their motivational effectiveness.

When all of this takes place, we tend to distort what's happening in the present. Small problems appear huge and gigantic. Simple difficulties seem terribly complex. Temporary struggles appear endless. We have difficulty seeing "light at the end of the tunnel."

Principle 4. It's God's plan that we get sufficient rest and relaxation to be able to handle life's challenges on the long haul.

There are times we are called upon to exert unusual amounts of physical and emotional energy. But if we do not take time to rest, eventually we'll lose ground and our efforts will become counterproductive.

I'm reminded of two men who started a journey across the great northland with two separate dog teams. One driver decided to stop and rest his dogs every seventh day. The other man decided to drive his dogs straight through.

At the end of the first week, one of the men—as planned—stopped his team and rested all that day. The other man continued to travel. By the end of the next week, the man who had rested his dogs, nearly caught up with the man who traveled straight through. But again, he stopped to rest his team on the seventh day.

By the end of the third week, the one who had rested his team had passed the man who traveled straight through—and in the end reached the final destination far ahead.

All of us need rest and recuperation. This is part of God's plan for all of us. Though we are not under Old Testament law, the principles still apply. Experience verifies it.

Principle 5. We are more vulnerable to satanic attacks when we are physically and psychologically exhausted.

It was not an accident that Satan tempted Christ in the wilderness *after* He had fasted for forty days and nights. Jesus was hungry and weak. It was then Satan made his move (see Matt. 4:1–11)! It should not surprise us then that Satan strikes us when we are weak physically and emotionally. It's doubly important that we be on guard during these periods of intense stress.

Principle 6. *Understanding these principles regarding depression will help us to cope with its presence and its affects in our lives.*

Nothing intensifies and complicates depression more than worry. When we are feeling anxiety over depression itself, we're actually adding to the problem that may have caused our depression in the first place. When we accept our depression as a reality, it helps us to overcome it.

As we'll see, however, Elijah needed more than food and rest. He also needed more than just insight. In our next chapter, we'll look at how God continued His "counseling process" with His servant Elijah.

Today, we're fortunate to understand far more about depression and its causes, as well as the way in which it can be treated. The facts are that most depression—even chemical depression—has deeper roots that have interfered with our body chemistry. Consequently, we need to discover what these roots are—which, more often than not, are related to stress.

Personally, I believe Elijah's depression was not so much "chemical" but as a result of physical and psychological exhaustion combined with spiritual disillusionment. From his human perspective, all that he had sacrificed for three and a half years seemed to be in vain.

The principles for overcoming depression that we can glean from the way God dealt with Elijah are basic in helping us overcome any kind of depression. Though the struggles that cause depression in our lives may be quite different from Elijah's problems, these principles are very basic in treating this kind of problem. It gives us a basic strategy and starting point for overcoming our own problems.

If, however, you have applied these principles over a period of time and have not gotten relief, you should seek medical advice from a competent doctor—preferably a Christian psychiatrist who understands our total makeup: physically, psychologically, and spiritually.

Becoming a Mature Man Emotionally

Read the following statements regarding depression. Understanding them will help us cope with the presence and affects of depression in our lives. Have you gotten any special insights from these statements? Write out a specific goal for the one you relate to the most, such as: "I will be aware that next time I have a 'mountain top' experience depression may follow. I will ask the Lord to help me respond with positive thoughts."

Statements

- Depression often follows "mountaintop experiences."
- Depression often follows intense periods of stress and hyperactivity.
- Depression often coincides with physical and emotional exhaustion.
- Depression often follows keen disappointment and disillusionment.
- Depression often results from periods of anger, particularly if we don't deal with it properly.
- Being a dedicated Christian who is used of God in significant ways does not guarantee that we'll not experience depression.
- Under certain circumstances, Christians should expect to experience depression and its accompanying results.
- Depression always distorts our view of reality.
- It's God's plan that we get sufficient rest and relaxation to be able to handle life's challenges on the long haul.
- We are more vulnerable to satanic attacks when we are physically and psychologically exhausted.

Set a Goal

With God's help, I will begin immediately to carry out the following goal in my life:

_____

_____

_____

_____

Memorize the Following Scripture

Come to me, all you who are weary and burdened, and I will give you rest.

MATTHEW 11:28

Chapter 10

God's Counseling Model
Read 1 Kings 19:9–18

*T*oday there are many theories regarding how to counsel people who have personal problems. Some people believe in being very directive—not mincing words, telling the person what he needs to do to overcome his inner struggles. Other people are more non-directive—emphasizing the importance of listening to people ventilate and verbalize, assuming they'll come up with their own solutions.

Both approaches represent an either/or position. Actually, at times people just need someone to listen. At other times, they need a lot of direction. And in most instances, people struggling with problems need both a sympathetic listening ear as well as good information as to how to solve their problems.

It takes a great deal of wisdom to maintain this balance. In dealing with Elijah's depression, God gives us a beautiful model. Though the Lord's approach in this particular set of circumstances doesn't cover all "counseling bases"—even the various types of depression—the Lord does give us a model that yields some powerful principles that will help us maintain balance in a variety of counseling situations.

Have You Had a Physical Lately?

The first thing the Lord did to help Elijah overcome his depression was to help him recuperate physically. We're not told how much time elapsed while he ate and slept in the wilderness of Beersheba. However, we do know that following his second meal, Elijah "traveled forty days and forty nights until he reached Horeb, the mountain of God" (1 Kings 19:8).

Elijah's Problems Were More Than Physical

Often when we study this passage—which deals with Elijah's depression—we stop with his physical recuperation, assuming that his psychological problems were solved. In reality, that's not the case.

Our first clue that Elijah was still depressed relates to how long it took him to make the trip from Beersheba to Horeb. The total distance is about two hundred miles. Elijah averaged only five miles a day. Had he been emotionally motivated, he could have made the trip in a week!

What a contrast between the man who ran twenty miles ahead of Ahab's chariot from Mount Carmel to Jezreel, and the man who is now trudging along through the wilderness headed for Mount Horeb. He no doubt looked like a man with the weight of the world on his shoulders. Previously, he had been buoyed up with excitement and anticipation. Now, Elijah was burdened down with sadness and a heavy heart. Though he had been strengthened physically from the food and rest in Beersheba, he was still feeling down emotionally. His depression had not lifted.

The Lord's First Counseling Session

When Elijah arrived at Horeb, he went into a cave and spent the night. And while there, God once again spoke to him: "What are you doing here, Elijah?" the Lord asked. "I have been very zealous for the LORD God Almighty. The Israelites have rejected your covenant, broken down your altars, and put your prophets to death with the sword. I am the only one left, and now they are trying to kill me too" (vv. 9–10).

Realities

Elijah *had* been "zealous for the LORD God Almighty."

➤ He had boldly confronted Ahab regarding the coming drought.

➤ He had been faithful to God during the long, lonely period of waiting in the ravine of Kerith.

➤ He had laid his own reputation on the line when he prayed for the widow's son to be restored to life.

➤ He had obeyed God's charge to meet Ahab and the false prophets on Mount Carmel.

No one would deny these realities. Indeed, Elijah *had* "been *very* zealous for the LORD God Almighty." Elijah was also accurate regarding Israel's sins. They had rejected God's covenant, had broken down the Lord's altars, and had put the Lord's prophets to death.

Distortions

There was one major reality Elijah couldn't grasp. He was not "the only one left" who hadn't forsaken the Lord. What about his friend, Obadiah? And what about the one hundred prophets Obadiah had hidden?

Elijah's response illustrates a very normal symptom associated with severe depression. Negative experiences block out positive realities. We focus on the facts that discourage us. Those that should be encouraging elude us.

This was Elijah's problem. He was so depressed he couldn't see beyond the dark clouds of despair that shrouded his weary soul.

God Listened

Food and rest helped Elijah recuperate physically. However, he also needed an opportunity to share how he felt—openly and honestly—without being judged and corrected. God listened to Elijah's feelings. In fact, the Lord made it easy for him to ventilate by asking him the question "What are you doing here, Elijah?" (19:9). Even though God knew what was in his heart, He also knew that Elijah needed to get his feelings out in the open. But even "talking" about his problem was not enough.

The Lord's Counsel

Elijah needed more than rest, nourishment, and an opportunity to ventilate his feelings in order to overcome his depression. Had he been experiencing a simple "downer"—as a lot of us do periodically—it may have worked. But Elijah's problem was much more complex. He needed spiritual and psychological insight; in fact, he needed some theological input and clarification. This is why the Lord instructed him to come out of the cave and to "stand on the mountain" in His presence (v. 11).

"The LORD was not in the wind." God's first step was to unleash the fury of a "great and powerful wind." It was so strong it literally ripped the landscape apart. Huge rocks cascaded down the mountain as if they were pebbles. At the same time, the Lord made it very clear to Elijah that He "was not in the wind" (v. 11).

"The LORD was not in the earthquake." The Lord followed the storm with an earthquake. Perhaps it was similar to the time God revealed His presence at Mount Sinai causing the whole mountain to tremble violently (see Exod. 19:18). But again the Lord made it clear to Elijah that He was not in this particular earthquake (see 1 Kings 19:11c).

"The LORD was not in the fire." The Lord followed the wind and the earthquake with a great fire—reminiscent of what He had just done on Mount Carmel in response to Elijah's prayer. But again we read that "the LORD was not in the fire" (v. 12a).

If He was not in the wind, the earthquake, or the fire, where was He? He was there, of course! He caused these things to happen. In fact, Elijah was also listening to His voice. But this time, God's personal presence appeared as "a gentle whisper" or a quiet rustling (v. 12b).

God's Second Counseling Session

Following this amazing demonstration of God's power, as well as revealing His presence in the gentle, whispering wind, the Lord once again repeated His question: "What are you doing here, Elijah?" Elijah answered, "I have been very zealous for the Lord God Almighty. The Israelites have rejected your covenant, broken down your altars, and put your prophets to death with the sword. I am the only one left, and now they are trying to kill me too" (vv. 13b–14).

The Lord's second question was the same as His first one. And so was Elijah's response. We see no outward evidence of any inward change. Depression and self-preoccupation continued to dominate Elijah's personality. In fact, it appears that God's powerful demonstration on the mountain made little impact on Elijah. But when Elijah heard the "gentle whisper," he was curious. We read that "he pulled his cloak over his face and went out and stood at the mouth of cave" (v. 13).

The Lord's Counsel

Though Elijah's thinking was still distorted, the Lord built on his positive response to the "gentle whisper," minor though it was. He helped Elijah get in touch with reality as well as with his feelings. God assured him he was not alone. In fact, there were "seven thousand in Israel"—all had "not bowed down to Baal" (v. 18). He was not the only prophet left, nor was he the only person who was still worshiping the one true God.

The Lord broadened Elijah's perspective even more by telling him that he never expected him to bear Israel's problems all by himself. There were other men who would help him—Hazael, Jehu, and a man who was to have a very special place in Elijah's life: his successor, Elisha (vv. 15–17).

Becoming God's Man Today

Principles to Live By

We can learn some powerful principles from the way God dealt with Elijah's depression. We can also apply these principles directly to our own lives and we can use them in helping others who are in a depressed state.

Principle 1. Physical exhaustion can contribute significantly to depression.

God created all of us as physical, psychological, and spiritual beings. Furthermore, these three dimensions in our personalities are intricately interrelated. When we are not feeling well *physically*, it invariably affects us psychologically and spiritually. When we are experiencing *psychological* stress, it will affect us physically and spiritually. And if we're having *spiritual* problems, we shouldn't be surprised if we have physical and psychological problems as well.

All of these factors were involved in Elijah's experience. Understandably, he was exhausted physically. His psychological stress had been overwhelming—not only on Mount Carmel but for a lengthy period of time. In his weakened condition, he lost his spiritual and theological perspectives when Ahab and Jezebel did not respond positively to what God had done on Mount Carmel.

God began the process of healing in Elijah's life by restoring him physically. This is where we should look first when we're dealing with depression—either in ourselves or in others. Though physical exhaustion may not be the major cause of the problem, it is always the place to begin. If it is the basic cause, we'll experience immediate relief once we have been restored physically. However, if it is not the major cause of depression, it is much easier to handle the real causes when we are physically healthy.

Spiritual Symptoms—Physical Causes

Over the years, I've had that unique opportunity to serve as both a professor and pastor. I remember theological students who have come to me over the years with terrible feelings of doubt regarding their Christian faith. In actuality, they were feeling terribly guilty and depressed because they believed that they were totally unspiritual for having these feelings. After all, they were preparing for the ministry and they had lost all motivation to pray, to read the Bible, and to go to church.

In almost all cases, they were exhausted physically and emotionally. They'd been "burning the candle" at both ends. Their minds were overloaded with biblical and theological truth. They were just plain tired.

I'll never forget the relief that showed on their faces and the peace that flooded their souls when I advised them to take several Sundays off and simply rest—not even to open their Bibles or even try to pray. They'd been doing that all week.

Before you judge my counsel too quickly, listen to what happened! In a very short time—often the very next week—they came to my office all smiles. Their doubts were gone! Their love for God at the "feeling level" had returned. Their motivation to serve God was back. Why? They needed physical and emotional rest and recuperation.

Chemical Depression

In an earlier chapter, I mentioned a businessman who was terribly depressed—a condition that was diagnosed as chemical depression. In instances like this, extreme stress over a prolonged period of time can interfere with chemical balances. Fortunately, medical science has discovered drugs that can often help restore these chemical balances rather quickly. They're called "anti-depressants" and if they're used properly, they help a depressed person to deal much more quickly and realistically with the psychological factors that caused the depression in the first place. It used to take years and complete rest for the body to restore these balances on its own. Thankfully, anti-depressants can often restore these balances in a matter of months, enabling the person to continue to live a normal life during the process and, at the same time, to deal with the root problems. Medical science is indeed a blessing from God—and we should not ignore it.

Principle 2. All of us need opportunities to ventilate our negative feelings in a nonjudgmental setting.

Being able to talk about our feelings openly and honestly (but responsibly) in a nonjudgmental setting is a very important step in dealing with depression. Just feeling accepted by someone we trust often can work miracles in helping us overcome our feelings of anxiety.

God Is Always *Listening*

No matter what we're feeling, God always has a listening ear. He is not waiting to pounce on us and condemn us when we share our feelings with Him—negative though they may be. He understands and cares. If He didn't, He would not wait until we share our feelings to discipline us because He already knows what they are.

Human Interaction

Elijah had a very unique relationship with God. Communication went both ways. They communicated as friend to friend.

Today, of course, God speaks to us through His Word, and we can speak to Him in prayer. However, as human beings we need another human being who can listen and interact with us. This is why the concept of the body of Christ is so important. We need other Christians in our lives to help us experience emotional and spiritual healing (see Rom. 12:4–5).

Responsible Verbalization

There are times when we need to pour out our feelings just as we did as children. However, prolonged expressions of anger and frustration can become irresponsible very quickly. Rather than helping us to resolve the problem, it only entrenches us in our negative feelings. To be specific, we do not have to stomp our feet, scream, and use foul language to express psychological distress. We can pour out our feelings openly, honestly, and intensely—but responsibly—just as Elijah did. On the other hand, if a distraught person loses control and becomes irresponsible and resorts to infantile expressions of anger, a mature counselor will not become judgmental and condemning but will sensitively and firmly lead this person to respond honestly in a mature and responsible way.

Principle 3. To overcome depression, we must understand and face reality.

Most of Elijah's thoughts were accurate, but some were not. Those thoughts that were inaccurate contributed significantly to his depression. Elijah needed to hear the facts that were eluding him. God firmly but lovingly communicated those facts.

Developing Objectivity

Remember that God didn't instruct Elijah until He had first given His servant opportunity to ventilate his feelings— not once, but twice. This process helped Elijah to develop objectivity. Keep in mind, however, that God did not allow Elijah to repeat himself over and over again before He set the record straight.

This is a very important point! Persistent verbal repetition does not solve emotional problems. In fact, if we repeat inaccuracies long enough, we tend to convince ourselves we're right. We become even more entrenched in an unreal world. In short, there comes a time when we need to stop verbalizing and listen to what others have to say. We must then act on that reality.

If you're going to a counselor who time after time listens to you repeat your problems without correcting your point of view, you're wasting your time! And if you're paying for the service, you're wasting your money!

Principle 4. Inaccurate theological perspectives can contribute significantly to depression.

Intricately interwoven throughout God's counseling approach with Elijah were several significant theological lessons—lessons that will help all of us maintain our spiritual and emotional equilibrium.

Lesson #1

God's normal ways of communicating with His children are not revelational and oriented toward the dramatic and phenomenal. This theological lesson *focuses on God Himself.* More specifically, Elijah was learning that windstorms, earthquakes, and lightning bolts are not God's normal ways of revealing Himself. It's true that God always maintains sovereign control over all natural phenomena. But it's also true that God doesn't always speak directly through these natural upheavals and reveal His presence as He did at Mount Sinai, on Mount Carmel, and as He will surely do when His judgments fall on the earth in the great tribulation period described in the Book of Revelation (see Rev. 6:12–14; 8:1–9).

God taught Elijah that His normal ways of revealing Himself are gentle, quiet ways. In fact, God is *always* present in this way. This was one of the theological lessons that God was teaching Elijah—and us!

Lesson #2

God's normal ways of relating to His children are not extensively experiential. This theological lesson *focuses on us.* In Elijah's case, it focused on his religious experience. He had come to expect the dramatic, the miraculous, the phenomenal! God sent ravens to bring him bread and meat every morning and every evening while he was in the Kerith Ravine. The jug of oil and the jar of meal in the widow's home never ran dry. He saw a dead boy restored to life. And when he prayed, fire fell from heaven on the sacrifice on Mount Carmel. And following that great dramatic event, God responded to his prayers with terrifying winds and torrential rains.

Don't misunderstand! God *was* present and speaking in a very specific way through *all* of these supernatural events. But Elijah—being "a man just like us"—had apparently come to depend upon those "emotionally moving" experiences to affirm God's presence in his life and ministry.

God does not normally reveal Himself in this way. During most of recorded history, God has revealed Himself in a "gentle whisper." As we've observed in chapter 8, there were significant periods when He became *very* dramatic—but always within a relatively short period of time. Once He had revealed His message, He continued to speak through what He had already revealed in supernatural, phenomenal ways.

As Christians, we must not come to rely on this kind of experience—experience that we believe is a direct revelation from God. If we do, we can feel as if God has forsaken us when we're not experiencing "emotional highs." Furthermore, we may confuse normal psychological experiences with what we believe are God's special messages to us. When this happens, we can become theologically and emotionally confused.

Lesson #3

God's normal ways of dealing with His children are not with persistent, external judgments. This theological lesson focuses on *God's grace.* It's true that His hand of judgment and punishment has fallen in severe ways at various moments in history. However, this has never happened until God's patience has been pushed to the limits. Even then, God has been quick to relent if people repented.

Some believe that Elijah's anger had taken over after the Mount Carmel experience, leaving him very disturbed over the fact that God continued to tolerate Israel's idolatry and sinful behavior. If this is true, God was teaching Elijah that His ways are gentle and long-suffering, not bombastic and given to quick judgments and punishment for sin.

This may be an accurate interpretation of what God was attempting to teach Elijah. If so, it certainly correlates with what we read about God's grace toward all men and women. As Peter stated, "The Lord is not slow in keeping his promise, as some understand slowness. *He is patient with you,* not wanting anyone to perish, but everyone to come to repentance" (2 Pet. 3:9).

Lesson #4

   God is never dependent on one person alone to accomplish His goals. This lesson focuses on *God's leadership plan.* No individual is strong enough physically, psychologically, or spiritually to handle God's work alone. Elijah needed to learn that lesson.

   It's easy to see why Elijah fell into this trap. After all, God had placed a very heavy burden on his shoulders. To a great extent, he had to stand alone during the three-and-a-half-year drought. But even then, there was Obadiah and others who had stood true to God.

   When we look at the way God accomplished His work through biblical history, we see that Moses needed Aaron. Later, Joshua needed Caleb. The apostle Paul needed Barnabas and Silas, and later Timothy and Titus. Peter needed John. As we'll see in our next chapter, Elijah needed Elisha.

   It's clear! God has never expected one man or woman to bear the complete burden of any ministry. For that matter, God doesn't even expect any one of His children to live the Christian life in isolation. We all need other Christians in our lives to encourage and help us.[1]

Becoming a Responsible Man

The following questions will help you to evaluate your life in the light of the principles we've just looked at in this chapter. Pray and ask the Holy Spirit to impress on your heart one lesson you need to apply more effectively in your life. Then write out a specific goal. For example, you may not be taking good care of yourself physically. You know you're eating too much "junk food" and you're not exercising on a regular basis.

1. Am I keeping myself in good physical condition—eating right, getting enough rest, exercising properly, etc.? When was the last time I had a complete and thorough physical examination?

2. Do I have a close friend or counselor with whom I can share my deepest feelings of anxiety, fear, anger, etc.? Does this person listen empathetically and nonjudgmentally?

3. When I share my feelings, is the person who is listening helping me face reality? Do I even let that person help me face reality?

4. Do I have a correct theological perspective on my personal problems? For example:

   ➤ Am I waiting for God to speak to me in some unique way when He has already spoken through His Word and through my Christian friends and personal circumstances?

   ➤ Am I relying too much upon experience in my Christian life, expecting the abnormal, the miraculous, the unusual? Am I relying more upon my feelings than correct doctrine and biblical truth?

   ➤ Do I allow myself to get overly involved emotionally in other people's failures and problems, causing depression in my own life?

   ➤ Am I taking too much responsibility on myself, not allowing others to bear the burden with me? Do I realize that God expects me to function only within the bounds of my human limitations—and that beyond this, God is ultimately responsible and in control?

Set a Goal

With God's help, I will begin immediately to carry out the following goal in my life:

_____

_____

_____

_____

Memorize the Following Scripture

Humble yourselves, therefore, under God's mighty hand, that he may lift you up in due time. Cast all your anxiety on him because he cares for you.

1 PETER 5:6–7

Chapter 11

We All Need a Friend

Read 1 Kings 19:12–21 and 2 Kings 2:1–14

*A*n English publication offered a prize for the best definition of a friend, and among the thousands of answers received were the following:

"One who multiplies joys, divides grief."

"One who understands our silence."

"A volume of sympathy bound in cloth."

"A watch which beats true for all time and never runs down."

But here is the definition that won the prize: *"A friend is one who comes in when the whole world has gone out!"*

If Elijah suddenly stepped into our world and described what happened following his mountaintop experience on Mount Carmel, he would certainly agree with this prize-winning definition. Elaborating, he might say, "When my whole world turned black as midnight, God brought Elisha into my life to be my friend."

This was God's final step in helping Elijah overcome his depression—the theme in this chapter.

But First, Let's Review

God had already dealt with Elijah's depression in four very practical ways.

1. He ministered to him physically with food and rest.
2. He gave Elijah the opportunity to ventilate his feelings in a nonjudgmental setting.
3. God helped His faithful prophet face reality—to get his facts straight.
4. He clarified his theological perspectives.

God's fifth step was the most practical of all. He brought Elisha into Elijah's life to be his friend and constant companion.

While God was helping Elijah regain perspective, He had already mentioned Elisha by name. God had chosen him to join Elijah in dealing with Israel's sin (see 1 Kings 19:17). But God had another purpose in choosing Elisha to serve with Elijah. Not only would he assist him in the ministry but he would become a faithful "attendant" and, most of all, a true friend (v. 21).

A Faithful Attendant

The Scriptures don't tell us what God said to Elijah regarding the way in which He was to choose Elisha. We simply read that when he left Mount Horeb, he "went from there and found Elisha son of Shaphat" (v. 19).

A Farm Boy

Elisha lived in the Jordan valley, far north and east of Mount Horeb, in a place called Abel Meholah (v. 16). His father was no doubt a well-to-do farmer. When Elijah first saw Elisha, he was working with eleven other men—each plowing with a yoke of oxen.

Apparently Elisha was not surprised by Elijah's sudden appearance. Along with most everyone in Israel, he had heard about this feisty old prophet who had confronted Ahab and the prophets of Baal on Mount Carmel.

The moment Elijah saw Elisha, he knew this was the man who was to become his attendant—and eventually his successor. Elijah approached Elisha and "threw his cloak around him." With this symbolic act, Elisha knew that God had called him to be a special helper and assistant to this great prophet in Israel. Without hesitation, he left his duties and his family to become Elijah's assistant.

No Turning Back

Elijah demonstrated his commitment to this high task by slaughtering his yoke of oxen and using his plowing equipment to cook the meat. At the same time, he invited his friends, neighbors, and fellow workers to join him in a farewell feast.

Elisha literally "burned his bridges" behind him. There was no turning back—no conflict of interest from this point forward. Elisha was totally committed to Elijah and the God they both served.

Anyone who is a leader knows how important it is to have associates and assistants you can trust. The more difficult the task, the more important it becomes to have people helping you that are totally trustworthy. It's important to any leader's personal well-being—physically, psychologically, and spiritually. Part of God's healing process for Elijah's depression involved this very thing. He provided Elijah with a dedicated and faithful man who could help him carry his burden—a man Elijah could trust implicitly.

Meet the Old Elijah

We're not told how long these two men traveled and ministered together. However, something very important happened immediately to Elijah. His depression subsided when Elisha joined the team. You see him once again responding positively to God's commands and without hesitating; he confronted the sins of idolatry at high levels in Israel (see 2 Kings 1:3–4). Drawing upon God's power, he worked miracles (see vv. 10–14) and he brought judgment on Israel's leaders because of their failure to turn to God. Clearly, Elijah's bout with depression was behind him.

A Personal Reflection

Elijah's experience at this moment in his life reminded me of a time in my own experience when I faced heavy-duty depression. Mine related to disillusionment. Several Christian leaders that I admired greatly had let me down. Unquestionably, there was inconsistency in their lives.

As a result, I got my own eyes off the Lord and began to doubt the reality of my Christian faith. There didn't seem to be anyone available that I could trust with my deep feelings of anxiety, fear, and depression.

At the time, I was still single, and the person who had been my roommate had moved on to another location. There were days in my life when I felt God had forsaken me. When I tried to pray, I felt as if God was nowhere to be found. I couldn't even read the prayers of David and feel that the Lord was listening.

Then one day another single man became my roommate. He was a committed Christian. He was sensitive, open, and caring. When I arrived home at night, there was always someone to talk to. Trust developed between us. I was able to share some of my deepest feelings.

As I reflect, this was a definite turning point in my life in overcoming my depression. Loneliness is lethal when we're already depressed. This is why we need other members of the body of Jesus Christ in our lives. What happened to me is not surprising! It happened to Elijah when he met Elisha.

A Loyal Friend

The time came when Elijah's work on earth was finished. But rather than let His servant die a natural death, the Lord decided to take him home to glory—"in a whirlwind" (2 Kings 2:1). Elijah's home-going was as dramatic as the events that characterized his life!

When Elijah planned to visit a group of prophets on three different occasions in three different locations, he asked Elisha to stay behind. We're not told what Elijah's motivation was in issuing these commands. Perhaps it was because he knew his time was short and he didn't want to worry his friend. However, Elisha would not hear of it. Notice his adamant response in the dialogue that follows:

ELIJAH'S COMMANDS	ELISHA'S RESPONSES
"Stay here; the LORD has sent me to Bethel" (v. 2a).	"I will not leave you" (v. 2b).
"Stay here, Elisha; the LORD has sent me to Jericho" (v. 4a).	"I will not leave you" (v. 4b).
"Stay here; the LORD has sent me to the Jordan" (v. 6a).	"I will not leave you" (v. 6b).

Elisha was not only Elijah's faithful attendant, he had become his loyal friend. Evidently, Elisha knew that Elijah was about to leave him and he was determined to stay by his side until that moment when they would be separated.

Jesus once said to His disciples—just before He went to the cross—"Greater love has no one than this, that he lay down his life for his friends. . . . I no longer call you servants, because a servant does not know his master's business. Instead, *I have called you friends,* for everything that I learned from my Father I have made known to you" (John 15:13–15).

Jesus called His disciples to be His servants. But as they worked together, ate together, and shared many other experiences, they developed a deeper and more meaningful relationship than merely "master and servant." They became true friends. Jesus had shared with them the most intimate details of His life and His purpose in coming to earth. They now knew "His business."

No Longer Alone

Elisha developed this kind of relationship with Elijah. Consequently, he ministered in a special way to this old prophet.

For three and a half years, Elijah had carried the burden God had laid on his shoulders virtually by himself. For at least a year, he was literally alone as he hid from Ahab in the Kerith Ravine.

Loneliness in itself causes depression—no doubt a basic factor in Elijah's difficult experience. True, with the exception of his year in isolation, he was often around other people. But they had not become his friends—at least not like Elisha.

I remember well the summers I spent in New York City working on my doctorate at New York University. Because I couldn't afford what it would cost to take my family with me, I had to leave my wife, Elaine, and my children at home—at that time in Wheaton, Illinois.

I spent many lonely days and nights without my family and other close friends. Weekends seemed to be the worst. I remember one Sunday afternoon particularly, walking through Washington Square Park. People were everywhere—talking, laughing, playing games, and enjoying other activities with one another. Though I was in the midst of a crowd of literally thousands, I never felt so all alone! For one thing, my best friend—my wife—was a thousand miles away. It was definitely depressing.

"The Two of Them Walked On"

Elijah needed a friend and Elisha became that friend! He became a man with whom Elijah could share the deepest and most intimate details of his life without fear of rejection, misinterpretation, or betrayal.

Elisha was always loyal to Elijah—a true test of friendship. Knowing the time was soon coming when they would be "temporarily" separated, Elisha would not leave his friend, even when Elijah asked him to stay behind. "I will not leave you," Elisha responded. And, "so the two of them walked on" together (2 Kings 2:6). And so it is with friends. They are loyal to each other and they "walk on" together no matter what the difficulties and problems in life.

A True Disciple

There's another dimension to this wonderful relationship that must have been very encouraging to Elijah. Elisha became a true disciple, eager to learn everything he could from his friend and mentor. He wanted to be prepared to carry on Elijah's prophetic ministry. I'm convinced Elisha's eagerness to learn also helped Elijah to forget about his feelings of disillusionment and despair.

"Let Me Inherit a Double Portion of Your Spirit"

Elisha knew he could never take over Elijah's powerful position in Israel without supernatural help. The moment came one day for Elisha to share *his feelings*. Elijah asked him what he could do for him before he was taken away. Without hesitation, Elisha responded, "Let me inherit a double portion of your spirit" (v. 2:9).

Don't misunderstand! Elisha was not asking that he be twice as successful as Elijah but that he be doubly blessed so he could measure up to Elijah's accomplishments. Elisha felt he would need twice the motivation and faith that Elijah had—just to keep up with his friend's level of achievement in God's kingdom.

This was not a selfish request! Elisha was not seeking to rise to stardom and become greater than Elijah. Just the opposite was true. He knew he could never fill this man's shoes in his own strength. Because his motives were pure, God granted his request.

"My Father! My Father!"

The moment eventually came when these two great friends were separated. As Elijah disappeared into heaven in a whirlwind, riding in a "chariot of fire" pulled by "horses of fire," Elisha cried out, "My father! My father!" (vv. 11–12).

In God's sight, Elijah and Elisha were brothers. They were spiritually equal. But from another point of view, they were not equals. They were separated by age and experience. Elisha was a son who looked to his father for guidance and help. He was a true disciple.

"As a Son with His Father"

The apostle Paul and Timothy had a similar relationship in the New Testament era. In fact, the parallels are uncanny. Paul called young Timothy to join him as his fellow missionary—in actuality, to become his attendant (see Acts 16:1–5). While they traveled together leading people to Christ and planting churches, they became very close friends. When Paul wrote to the Philippians, he described the mutual trust and confidence that existed between the two of them. Writing from a Roman prison, Paul said:

> "I hope in the Lord Jesus to send Timothy to you soon, that I also may be cheered when I receive news about you. I have no one else like him, who takes a genuine interest in your welfare. For everyone looks out for his own interests, not those of Jesus Christ. But you know that Timothy has proved himself, because *as a son with his father* he has served with me in the work of the gospel." (Phil. 2:19–22)

"My Son, Be Strong"

Paul, like Elijah, was destined to leave his ministry in the hands of one of his best friends. That man was Timothy. In the last letter he ever wrote before God took him home to heaven, he penned these words: "You then, *my son, be strong* in the grace that is in Christ Jesus. And the things you have heard me say in the presence of many witnesses entrust to reliable men who will also be qualified to teach others" (2 Tim. 2:1–2).

God's Work Must Go On!

As Paul faced the prospect of his own death, he was greatly encouraged to know that the work he started on earth would continue through Timothy—a faithful attendant, a loyal friend, and a true disciple.

The same kind of relationship encouraged Elijah. He knew he was going to leave the work in the hands of a faithful man who had learned everything he could while they served together. Because of this unique relationship, I'm convinced that Elijah never faced the same kind of depression ever again!

Becoming God's Man Today

Principles to Live By

The essence of the relationship that existed between Elijah and Elisha can be summarized with one major point—*friendship*. We all have acquaintances, and that's important. But we all need friends—those we can relate to at a deeper level. It's a God-created need—and a means for helping us maintain our emotional and spiritual equilibrium.

Principle 1. God designed the husband and wife relationship to be a friendship.

One of the most wonderful and beautiful statements any marital partner can make about the other is to say, "This is my best friend!" Unfortunately, many couples live together, but they are not close friends.

God wants all marital partners to become friends—close friends—two people who can share their lives together in a total sense. He wants them to become one—not just physically, but emotionally and spiritually. Obviously, this is a process that takes time and effort.

Boyfriend—Girlfriend

Too many couples enter marriage without first becoming friends. The relationship is often built more on physical and emotional attraction rather than on a growing relationship that reflects true friendship.

I've always admired the relationship my daughter, Robyn, developed with her husband, Bob, before they were married. During high school days and even throughout their college life, they were best friends! Fortunately, they had the opportunity to get to know each other on the ski slopes. Both families—ours and Bob's—got to know each other well and together, we spent time each year in the Colorado mountains. I remember how Bob and Robyn used to take off at the beginning of the day and ski together until the slopes closed. They were great buddies— and we later discovered that they were able to share at a very deep level long before they ever became romantically involved.

Eventually, they began to date. I remember Robyn sharing one day—after they had married—that she was initially afraid of dating Bob in a romantic way for fear that it might not work out and she might lose her best male friend!

Needless to say, what began as a great friendship resulted in marriage—and in an even deepening friendship. Perhaps the thing that I remember the most, however, is how this relationship affected Robyn's younger brother, Kenton. He admired what he saw, and that's what he wanted in his own dating relationship. Fortunately, God allowed that to happen to him as well.

Fortunately, couples can become friends after marriage. Indeed, it's never too late! However, those who become friends *before* they take the final step have a decided head start in developing the kind of relationship God intended.[1]

Principle 2. It's God's desire that our children grow up to be our best friends.

Our children can and should become our best friends. Usually this doesn't happen, of course, until our children get beyond the teen years. One of the most exciting things I hear is when my grown daughters tell others that they consider their mother their *best friend!* That one statement alone makes all of the previous years of parenting worth every minute.

Principle 3. Every couple needs a close friendship *with at least one other couple— and* good friendships *with several others.*

This kind of relationship happens when one couple reaches out to another. Remember, however, this takes time. Sometimes people do not respond because they already have close friends. They may also be convinced in their own minds that they don't need close friends—even though they do.

Sometimes couples do not respond because those reaching out to them are trying too hard. They appear to be possessive. In the process, they scare people off. If this is happening in your own relationships, seek advice from another mature couple as to how to approach this kind of effort with balance.

Remember, too, that some people who desperately need friends sometimes withdraw and give the impression they don't want friends! And sure enough, they don't find them because people misinterpret their reactions. We should be on the lookout for people who are resorting to what psychologists call "reaction formation." What they really want is not what they're communicating. In fact, the signal they're sending out is just the opposite of their hearts' desire. If you're able to discern this kind of behavior, you might be able to set people free to become what God wants them to become—and, in the process, to develop some deep friendships.

Principle 4. Every husband needs a close *male friend and other* good *female friends outside of the marital relationship; and every wife needs a* close *female friend and other* good *male friends outside of the marriage.*

This principle is worded very carefully. If you stop and think for a moment, you'll understand why. You see, it's dangerous for a husband to have a *close* female friend other than his wife. Furthermore, it's dangerous for a wife to have a *close* male friend who is not her husband. Unfortunately, there are some people in this world that advocate these kinds of relationships. Mark my word—this can be lethal! More than likely, it will destroy marriages.

Having issued this warning, it also needs to be stated that every husband needs *good* female friendships. Likewise, every wife needs *good* male friendships. This is normal, natural, and necessary. It's part of God's design for the body of Christ. Ironically, we can also destroy a marriage through jealousy. It's tragic when a wife becomes jealous of her husband's female friendships and a husband becomes jealous of his wife's male friendships. This indicates lack of trust. However, if either partner develops *close* friendships with the opposite sex, either partner has a right to be concerned!

Principle 5. Every unmarried person needs a close friend—hopefully more than one.

Though singles need close friends among both sexes, an opposite sex friendship among unmarried people can easily lead to illegitimate sexual behavior. This can happen naturally because of the way God created us. But it's happening much more frequently in our society because we have adopted a value system that contradicts the Bible. God says that sex outside of marriage is sinful. If we ignore God's laws, it will eventually lead to heartache, disillusionment, and God's discipline.

Often friendships among unmarried people become possessive and exclusive. This kind of relationship can easily destroy a friendship. This caution, of course, applies to every relationship described thus far—including husband/wife relationships and parent/child relationships.

Principle 6. All Christians are friends because of our unique relationship in Jesus Christ.

As Christians we have a common bond that goes beyond the dimensions of friendship that have just been described. Our relationships with one another are more than flesh and blood—

more than just feelings and emotions. Our relationships in Christ go beyond time spent with one another. We are friends because of our oneness in Jesus Christ.

I have sensed this on many occasions as I've ministered to Christians in other parts of the world. I have met total strangers, spent only a few hours together in spiritual communion, and when I leave I feel as if I had known these people for years. Our hearts have been very quickly bound together in love. Why? It's because of our spiritual relationship. It's because we're brothers and sisters in Jesus Christ. It's supernatural.

If this happens among Christians who have not known each other for a lengthy period of time, think what can happen when Christians get to know each other at a much deeper level!

Thoughts to Ponder

- ➤ "Some people make enemies instead of friends because it is less trouble." E. C. McKenzie
- ➤ "Be slow in choosing a friend, slower in changing." Benjamin Franklin
- ➤ "An old friend is better than two new ones." Russian Proverb
- ➤ "Associate yourself with men of good quality if you esteem your own reputation: for 'tis better to be alone than in bad company." George Washington
- ➤ "When we lose a friend we die a little."
- ➤ "If you really want to know who your friends are, just make a mistake." The Bible Friend
- ➤ "So long as we love we serve. No man is useless while he is a friend." Robert Louis Stevenson

Becoming a Man Who Is a True Friend

Evaluate the preceding principles and prayerfully ask the Holy Spirit to impress on your heart one lesson you need to apply more effectively in your life. Then write out a specific goal. For example, you may not have a close friend. One reason may be that you've never reached out to someone else. Or, you've not realized how important it is to have someone you can be close to.

Set a Goal

With God's help, I will begin immediately to carry out the following goal in my life:

_____

_____

_____

_____

Memorize the Following Scripture

Greater love has no one than this, that he lay down his life for his friends. You are my friends if you do what I command. I no longer call you servants, because a servant does not know his master's business. Instead, I have called you friends, for everything that I learned from my Father I have made known to you.

JOHN 15:13–15

Chapter 12

What Will People Remember?
Read 1 Kings 16:29–34; 17; 18; 19 and 2 Kings 2:1–14

When you and I come to the end of our lives on earth, what will people remember about us? That's a thought-provoking and convicting question—one that I wrestled with as I prepared this final chapter on Elijah's life.

More specifically, what will my children remember? What will my friends remember? What will my associates remember? What will those I've ministered to remember about my life? What will people remember about you?

Here are some *positive possibilities!*

➤ My success as a Christian parent?

➤ My commitment to the church?

➤ My business acumen?

➤ My ability to earn money?

➤ My unselfish spirit?

➤ My concern for others?

➤ My soul-winning efforts?

➤ My teaching and preaching ability?

➤ My diligence?

➤ My family?

➤ My organizational ability?

➤ My loving spirit?

➤ My patience?

➤ My faith?

➤ My knowledge of the Bible?

➤ My generous spirit?

Certainly all of these qualities are significant, noteworthy, and even praiseworthy! But is there something *more* significant and *more* noteworthy and *more* praiseworthy? I think so! Elijah's life shows us what it is!

Elijah stands out in biblical history as one of the most significant Old Testament prophets who ever lived. Why was he so uniquely used by God? What was the secret to his success?

There is no secret! The reasons jut out from the numerous events in his life as clearly as three protruding mountain peaks silhouetted against the evening sky. As the sun sets on this old prophet's life, we can look back and see three primary reasons why God used Elijah to accomplish His purposes in this world.

A Man of God

The story of Elijah's life certainly illustrates and verifies James' conclusion (see James 5:17). At times Elijah was terribly discouraged and very lonely. At other times he was filled with anxiety and intensely fearful and horribly disillusioned. He experienced deep depression—so much so that he wanted to die. But, in spite of his humanness, Elijah was a "man of God."

What an encouraging combination! In spite of his human weaknesses and failures, God still used him to do His work in this world.

Elijah was a *prophet of God,* who experienced the *power of God!* Because of this unique calling, he was often identified as a *man of God.*

The Widow's Witness

For example, after Elijah had prayed for the widow's son and then presented the boy alive, she responded, "Now I know that you are a *man of God*" (1 Kings 17:24). There was an obvious relationship between Elijah's ability to unleash God's supernatural power and the title the widow gave him.

Ahaziah's Question

Elijah's reputation preceded him—especially toward the end of his life. After Ahab had passed off the scene, his son Ahaziah ruled Israel. On one occasion he injured himself badly and sent messengers to consult a false god to try to discover if he was going to get well. At the same time, the Lord revealed to Elijah what Ahaziah was about to do and sent him to meet the king's messengers. "Is it because there is no God in Israel that you are going off to consult Baal-Zebub, the god of Ekron?" Elijah asked. "Therefore this is what the LORD says: 'You will not leave the bed you are lying on. You will certainly die!'"(2 Kings 1:3–4).

When Ahaziah's messengers returned and reported what Elijah had said, the king spontaneously asked a question—"What kind of man was it who came to meet you and told you this?" (v. 7).

Not knowing who Elijah was, the messengers identified him as "a man with a garment of hair and a leather belt around his waist." Immediately the king knew who had sent the message. "That was Elijah the Tishbite," the king responded (v. 8).

King Ahaziah identified Elijah for two reasons. First, he knew what he wore. But second, he knew his reputation as a "man of God" (v. 9). In fact, Azahiah sent his messengers back and told them to identify him with this title. Elijah's response startled everyone. "If I am a *man of God,*" Elijah responded, "may fire come down from heaven and consume you and your fifty men!" Sure enough, fire fell, verifying Elijah's unique relationship with God (v. 12). He was a "man of God" because of the "power of God" in his life.

Elijah Served the Living God

Elijah demonstrated who he was not only by *what he did,* but also by *what he said.* Clearly, there was only one God in his life—the God of Abraham, Isaac, and Jacob. When he first confronted Ahab regarding his sins of idolatry, Elijah stated immediately that he *served the living God* (see 1 Kings 17:1)—not idols of wood and stone. Three and a half years later—when conversing with his friend Obadiah—he made the same basic statement: "As the LORD Almighty lives, *whom I serve,* I will surely present myself to Ahab today" (18:15).

Those who knew Elijah, either personally or by reputation, knew he served a living God. Beyond anything else he wanted to honor God's name. He was so committed to the Lord he was willing to risk his own life. He would not compromise his convictions either in worship or in his lifestyle. With both, he demonstrated that he was a "man of God."

A Man of Prayer

Elijah's reputation as a "man of God" was definitely associated with his prayer life. In fact, this is what impressed James. Though he "was a man just like us," James wrote, yet, "he *prayed earnestly* that it would not rain. . . . Again he *prayed,* and the heavens gave rain, and the earth produced its crops" (James 5:17–18).

Every major miracle associated with Elijah's life was also associated with prayer. The three-and-a-half-year drought began and ended when Elijah prayed. The widow's son was healed when Elijah cried out for healing (see 1 Kings 17:17–23). Fire fell on Mount Carmel when he "stepped forward and prayed" (see 18:36–37). The connection is clear: man of God—man of prayer!

Pure Motives

There's a deeper lesson that we can learn about Elijah's prayer life. We must remember that he didn't just pray; he prayed with pure motives. When he asked the Lord to stop the rain, it was to demonstrate to Israel that *there was only one true God* (see 17:1). When he prayed that fire would fall from heaven to consume the sacrifice, it was to demonstrate to Israel who God was—but also how Elijah viewed himself. "Let it be known today that *you are God* in Israel and that *I am your servant* and have done all these things *at your command"* (18:36).

Elijah's motives in prayer were to let Israel know that it was God—the one true God—who answers prayer and demonstrates power. He also wanted everyone to know that he was just God's servant carrying out God's orders.

A Man of God's Word

There is a unique pattern that is repeated again and again in Elijah's life. First, God revealed His will to Elijah. Second, Elijah obeyed!

The Ravine of Kerith

> 1 Kings 17:2—"Then the word of the LORD came to Elijah"
> v. 5—"So he did what the LORD had told him."

The Widow in Sidon

> v. 8—"Then the word of the LORD came to him"
> v. 10—"So he went."

The Confrontation with Ahab

> 18:1—"The word of the LORD came to Elijah"
> v. 2—"So Elijah went."

The Call of Elisha

> 19:15—"The LORD said to him"
> v. 19—"So Elijah went."

The Messengers of King Ahaziah

2 Kings 1:3—"But the angel of the LORD said to Elijah"
v. 4—"So Elijah went."

The Confrontation with King Ahaziah

v. 15a—"The angel of the LORD said to Elijah"
v. 15b—"So Elijah got up and went."

The pattern is clear. Each time God told Elijah to do something, he responded. Though he went through a time of deep depression that temporarily affected his ability to respond to the Lord, eventually Elijah once again obeyed God's voice and experienced God's power and blessing in his life.

Becoming God's Man Today

Principles to Live By

Throughout this study of Elijah's life, we've gleaned a number of powerful principles to guide us in our own personal experiences. However, when all is said and done, there are three outstanding qualities that characterize this man. He was *a man of God, a man of prayer,* and *a man committed to obeying God's Word.* This is why Elijah stands tall in biblical history as one of the greatest prophets who ever lived.

Is it possible to be remembered in the same way as Elijah? The answer is definitely "yes" if we develop Elijah's perspective on life. True, he was a unique man—especially called and empowered by God.

> As a *man of God,* he was one of those special people who had access to God's power to work miracles.

> As a *man of prayer,* he was one of those unique people who saw God respond in very unusual ways.

> As a *man of God's Word,* he heard God speak to him directly on numerous occasions, revealing His specific will!

However, this unique calling, this unique power, this unique access to God does not mean we cannot be remembered in the same way.

Principle 1. We, too, can be men of God—men who reflect commitment to God and demonstrate His character and power in our lives.

We may not be able to work the same miracles as Elijah. This was God's specific plan for him. On the other hand, we must remember that it was this same supernatural power that saved us and that has given us eternal life (see Eph. 1:19–20). It's the same power that can strengthen us in our inner being "so that Christ may dwell in our hearts through faith" (3:17). It's also the same power that enables us "to grasp how wide and long and high and deep is the love of Christ, and to know this love that surpasses knowledge" that enables us to "be filled to the measure of all the fullness of God" (vv. 18–19). And we must never forget that wonderful doxology at the conclusion of Paul's prayers to the Ephesians: "Now to him who is able to do immeasurably more than all we ask or imagine, *according to his power that is at work within us,* to him be glory in the church and in Christ Jesus throughout all generations, for ever and ever! Amen" (vv. 20–21).

Principle 2. We, too, can be men of prayer, seeing God answer in unusual ways.

It's true that Elijah experienced phenomenal answers to prayer. This happened because he was praying in the will of God and with pure motives. But we must never forget that James reminds us of a promise that is enduring—"You do not have, because you do not ask God. When you ask, you do not receive, because you ask with wrong motives, that you may spend what you get on your pleasures" (James 4:2–3).

God still answers prayer today. The more we search the Word of God, the more we will discover the will of God—and, in turn, the more we will experience answers to prayer as we pray according to His divine will. Focus for a moment on the words of the apostle John: "This is the confidence we have in approaching God: that *if we ask anything according to his will,* he hears us. And if we know that he hears us—whatever we ask— we know that we have what we asked of him" (1 John 5:14–15).

Principle 3. We, too, can hear God's voice, clearly and precisely, as He has spoken through Scripture. Furthermore, we can choose to obey or disobey what He has said.

Stop and think for a moment. You and I can know more about God's will than most of the people we read about in the Bible. Even the great apostle Peter as well as the apostle Paul did not have access to the Scriptures as we do. However, God used these men in a very specific way—as well as all of the authors of Scripture—to give us a very clear picture of what God desires in our lives. Consider Paul's words to Timothy: "All Scripture is God-breathed and is useful for teaching, rebuking, correcting and training in righteousness, so that the *man of God* may be thoroughly equipped for every good work" (2 Tim. 3:16–17).

My Personal Encounter with a Man of God

Dr. William Culberson served as president of Moody Bible Institute for many years. When he died, Warren Wiersbe was asked to write his official biography. While researching his life, Wiersbe talked at length with his family and his close associates. He read through his correspondence and a number of his sermons. When he finally completed the manuscript telling the story of his life, the author chose the title of the book— *William Culberson—A Man of God!* The late Dr. Wilbur Smith who knew Culberson well, made this statement: "My first impression and a lasting one is that he is a *man of God.*"

Fortunately, I got to know Dr. Culberson very well when I served as a faculty member at Moody Bible Institute. Our close association lasted for thirteen years before I left to teach at Dallas Theological Seminary. During that time, I not only had opportunity to associate with Dr. Culberson as a member of the Moody faculty; I also had a unique opportunity for fellowship in athletics. We played together nearly ten years on the volleyball court, sometimes two or three times a week. About half the time, I played on his team. The other half, we were fierce competitors, playing opposite each other.

If you're athletic at all, you're well aware that it's at times like these that you really get to know another person. What we "really are" comes out under pressure. We both played very competitively, whether "with" or "against" each other. Following our games, we often talked at length since his locker was next to mine. We spent a lot of time in good-natured kidding and ribbing each other. At other times, our conversations were very serious.

When the book was published, those who knew Dr. Culberson well were not surprised at the title! It was an accurate description. Though he was a man just like any one of us—and I saw that often on the volleyball court—I never saw him violate his spiritual convictions. He could express his opinions as fiercely as I could over what we thought were bad calls, but if he ever thought he was out of order, he was quick to right the wrong!

Perhaps this is why I remember so well something he said in chapel one day. I was seated with the faculty—just beginning my teaching career at that time. Speaking with deep conviction, Dr. Culberson said to the students as he gestured toward those of us seated in the faculty section, "Young people, you will forget what these teachers *say*, but you will never forget what they *are!*"

Yes, this message was directed at the students! But the impact hit me full force—and I'm sure my fellow faculty members as well. His exhortation became even more meaningful to me in years to come against the backdrop of the way he lived his life.

Is this not what we remember about Elijah? Is this not what stands out in the record of his life? It was what he was as a man of God that highlights what he did. What he said only reflected his relationship with the God he served!

A Man of Resolve

During his lifetime, Jonathan Edwards, that great preacher and teacher, set forth five resolutions for his life:

1. "Resolve, to live with all my might while I do live.

2. "Resolve, never to lose one moment of time, to improve it in the most profitable way I can.

3. "Resolve, never to do anything which I should despise or think meanly of in another.

4. "Resolve, never to do anything out of revenge.

5. "Resolve, never to do anything which I should be afraid if it were the last hour of my life."

Becoming a Man of God, a Man of Prayer, and a Man of the Word

There are many valid ways to demonstrate spiritual convictions in our lives. But Elijah's example gives us three of the most basic resolutions that reflect God's will for every Christian man. As you read over the following three resolutions, pray and ask the Holy Spirit to strengthen you in the area where you perhaps are the weakest. Then write out a specific goal. For example, you may now recognize that you need to spend more time in the Word of God. You may also need to spend more time in prayer. Whatever your need, allow God to speak to your heart:

➤ I resolve to always be a *man of God*, putting Him first in all I do, never bringing His name and reputation into disrepute, and, by God's grace, always reflecting His righteousness.

➤ I resolve to be a *man of prayer,* never attempting to achieve goals in my own strength alone, but always seeking His guidance, His enabling, His divine assistance and help. And when He does answer, I will always give God the glory due His name.

➤ I resolve to be a *man of God's Word,* consistently learning more of what God says, interpreting it accurately, obeying the Lord's spiritual directives, and consistently applying His divine principles.

Set a Goal

With God's help, I will begin immediately to carry out the following goal in my life:

_____

_____

_____

_____

Memorize the Following Scripture

Not that I have already obtained all this, or have already been made perfect, but I press on to take hold of that for which Christ Jesus took hold of me. Brothers, I do not consider myself yet to have taken hold of it. But one thing I do: Forgetting what is behind and straining toward what is ahead, I press on toward the goal to win the prize for which God has called me heavenward in Christ Jesus.

PHILIPPIANS 3:12–14

Endnotes

Chapter 1

1. C. F. Keil, *Commentary on the Old Testament* (Grand Rapids: Wm. B. Eerdmans Publishing Co.), 3:229.

2. Robert Jamieson, *A Commentary on the Old and New Testaments* (Grand Rapids: Wm. B. Eerdmans Publishing Co., 1948), 2:348.

Chapter 2

1. Will H. Houghton, "By Life, or By Death" (Copyright 1938, by George S. Schuler).

2. F. Kefa Sempangi, *A Distant Grief* (Ventura, Calif.: Regal Books, 1979), 119–21.

Chapter 3

1. See *A Biblical Theology of Material Possessions* and *Real Prosperity,* both published by Moody Press and written by Gene Getz.

2. Charles Ryrie, *Balancing the Christian Life* (Chicago: Moody Press, 1969), 84.

3. F. Kefa Sempangi, *A Distant Grief* (Ventura, Calif.: Regal Books, 1979), 179–80.

Chapter 5

1. Since God's command for Elijah to go and see Ahab happened in the third year, and the encounter with the prophets of Baal was near at hand, after which it rained again, some commentators believe that the historical record in 1 Kings is calculated from the time Elijah went into hiding. In other words, the period before he fled to the ravine of Kerith is estimated to be about six months. There would then be another three years of drought, and God's command to go and see King Ahab would come in the third year, but probably at the end of that year. This calculation would then correspond to James' statement that the drought lasted for three and a half years (see James 5:17).

Chapter 7

1. Robert Jamieson, *A Commentary on the Old and New Testaments* (Grand Rapids: Wm. B. Eerdmans Publishing Co., 1948), 2:353.

Chapter 10

1. See *Building Up One Another* authored by Gene A. Getz and published by Victor Books (Wheaton, Ill.).

Chapter 11

1. To deepen your marital friendship, it is recommended that you study together *Partners for Life* by Gene Getz.